RECONSTRUCTION TO RESTORATION

DRY BONES

GOD'S PLAN FOR RESTORING MARRIAGE

RECONSTRUCTION TO RESTORATION

DRY BONES

GOD'S PLAN FOR RESTORING MARRIAGE

NYCHOLLE WOOLFOLK-GATER

HUNTER ENTERTAINMENT NETWORK

Colorado Springs, Colorado

To order products, or for any other correspondence:

Hunter Entertainment Network
4164 Austin Bluffs Parkway, Suite 214
Colorado Springs, Colorado 80918
www.hunter-ent-net.com
Tel. (253) 906-2160 – Fax: (719) 528-6359
E-mail: contact@hunter-entertainment.com
Or reach us on Facebook at: Hunter Entertainment Network
"Offering God's Heart to a Dying World"

This book and all other Hunter Entertainment Network™, Hunter Heart
Publishing™, and Hunter Heart Kids™ books are available at Christian
bookstores and distributors worldwide.

Chief Editor: Gord Dormer
Book cover design: Phil Coles Independent Design
Layout & logos: Exousia Marketing Group www.exousiamg.com

ISBN: 978-1-937741-28-0

Printed in the United States of America.

Dedication

Dedicated to past, present, and future shoulders I have stood on who spoke life to me when I could not see or want life. I am forever grateful. I can still hear the voice of my sister friend saying, "You can do this." I know my sister, I know my friend! To our spiritual counselors who helped us realize *one flesh*, you opened your homes to ensure we were properly counseled. You two are a living testimony of God's love and forgiveness. You helped us to plant seeds and we're reaping the harvest. To my life group sisters, our Tuesday night meetings were an answered prayer, the support and unadulterated love is forever engraved in my heart. My *Encounter* sisters, you were there when God spoke to me; your prayers ushered the voice of our sweet Savior as He spoke, "I have always been here, and I am here now." I have never felt so safe to be free, and empowered to be vulnerable in the presence of the Lord in all my life, thank you.

To my husband, Darrick E. Gater, a real man, a loving father, and my best friend. You have been the rock that has kept our family together; your unwavering love and protection has covered me when I was in dark places. Thank you for allowing me to share our story in black and white. Thank you for holding on even when I wanted so desperately for you to let go. Our journey has been dark and light, long and hard, but we have come out on the other side. I will give you the rest of my life.

To our children Brittany, Amber, Colby, Devin, Eugene, and Ben, and our grandbabies Kingston and Tristan, I hope we have shown you an example of love and a living testimony of God's grace and mercy. May you grow old with the man or woman of your youth and be blessed.

Introduction

First, let me begin by giving honor and glory to God! God is my refuge and strength, a very present help in trouble.

Psalm 46:1 (NKJV)

—— ❧ ❦ ——

This book is written for men and women. It's a book that challenges us to rethink our commitment; the covenant made the day we said, "I do" and became one. In the book of Genesis, the very first book in the Bible, God made Adam a help mate, formed from Adam's rib, and named her *woman* because she was taken from man. The Word says, "Therefore shall a man leave his father and his mother and shall cleave unto his wife: and they shall be of one flesh." Genesis 2:24 (KJV) I am not a Bible scholar or theologian; I am a woman who put on the whole armor of God, challenged my circumstances, stood on the Word of God, tried in the fire, and came out gold. This book will empower you with the Word of God, the scriptures we stood on to restore our marriage! This will allow you to have the tools necessary to make this union, your union, this covenant work! You made a covenant unto God to love, honor, and cherish as long as you both shall live; for better or worse; richer or poor; until death do you part. Do you remember this covenant? Do you truly understand what covenant means or one flesh? Merriam-Webster defines *covenant* as a formal, solemn and binding agreement. However, in biblical context, a covenant is, "a contract between two parties that is established before God as a witness, a contract whose permanence is ultimately safeguarded by God" according to Andreas Kostenberger.[i] The Word clearly explains One Flesh and God's purpose for your marriage.

Meditate on Malachi 2:15-16 (AMP):

"And did not God make [you and your wife] one [flesh]? Did not one make you and preserve your spirit alive? And why [did God make you two] one? Because He sought a godly offspring [from your union]. Therefore, take heed to yourselves, and let not one deal treacherously and be faithless to the wife of his youth. For the Lord, the God of Israel, says: I hate divorce and marital separation and him who covers his garment [his wife] with violence. Therefore keep a watch upon your spirit [that it may be controlled by My Spirit], that you deal not treacherously and faithlessly [with your marriage mate]."

This Scripture, I believe, exemplifies God's original intention within the union of marriage. God wants a godly offspring and He warns us to guard our spirit.

My prayer is that this book will empower you to:

• Restore your relationship with God, your first love. The center and head of your foundation must be God.

• Restore your covenant! This means acknowledging the power in the union of two and understand God's original plan for marriage.

• Understand One Flesh; you are not a creation of a sum, but a whole of one another

• Discover the "negative influence or spirit" in your home and relationship. Some people call these negative influences spirits, demons, or Satan. Any negative influence on the body by pressure, oppression, suggestion, or temptation would fall under this negative influence or spirit. This explanation is one I have used for some time during my studies. I am unsure if there is a person to credit for this during my many years of appearing in conferences and worship services. Remember, the devil is here to stop your purpose and heighten the influence of negative thinking to get you off your purpose. Satan is here for what I call the *Triple D Threat*: to deceive, discourage, and destroy.

- We serve a God that is Omnipresent, Omnipotent, and Omniscient. He is the Trinity.

- You will Recover all the enemy has stolen from you!

My Prayer For You

"We are all faced with a series of great opportunities brilliantly disguised as impossible situations." Charles R. Swindoll

Father God, I come before You as humble as I may, giving thanks unto You for the millions of marriages You will restore. I thank You for the guidance and protection of my brothers and sisters as they read this book. I ask for protection as they embark upon restoring what You have joined together. I ask You Father to bring into remembrance the day they were joined, and restore to them your definition of wholeness and a life as one. You told Ezekiel to prophesy to the dry bones and I am praying my brothers and sisters will prophesy to each other, change their speech, and channel their energy to restore life into their marriage. I ask that You do unto each reader what you have done to my marriage; restore, heal, and unify in the mighty name of Jesus, Amen.

Before we begin, you must be fully committed to working on your marriage. Below is a list of things I want you to commit to:

1. Expect restoration! When you enter into your place of worship; when you come with expectancy, you will always leave receiving something. You will get out of this what you actually put into it. This book was written and prayed over with expectancy of healing and restoration for each and every reader.

2. Commit the scriptures referenced to memory. Put on the whole armor of God (Ephesians 6:10-17). This book will help you to put on the whole armor by simply learning the Word of God, getting the Word in your Spirit, and applying the Word to your life. Luke 10:40-42 (KJV) states: "And Jesus answered and said unto her, Martha, Martha, thou art careful and troubled about many things: But one thing is needful: and Mary hath chosen that good part, which shall not be taken away from her." Isaiah 26:3 (KJV) says, "Thou wilt keep him in perfect peace, whose mind is stayed on thee: because he trusteth in thee."

3. I need you to devote 10% of your day to prayer and worship. Formula: 24 hours times 60 minutes (convert hours to minutes) 1440 minutes, 10% equals 144 minutes, this equates to 2 hours and 24 minutes of worship and prayer. Where do I get this basis from? Scripturally, the Word of God confirms in Malachi 3:10-11(KJV): "Bring ye all the tithes into the storehouse, that there may be meat in mine house, and prove me now herewith, saith the Lord of hosts, if I will not open you the windows of heaven, and pour you out a blessing, that there shall not be room enough to receive it. And I will rebuke the devourer for your sakes, and he shall not destroy the fruits of your ground; neither shall your vine cast her fruit before the time in the field, saith the Lord of Host." There is some significance to 10%. Our tithe, recognized by most churches, is typically 10%; anything over that amount is an offering. Someone needing to lose weight under the guidance of a medical doctor is educated on the health benefits of losing simply 10% of your weight. Financial planners will tell you to pay yourself first by saving 10% of your income. There's a common understanding that 10% shows significant benefits. Please understand

this 10% does not have to be completed in one sitting. I will never limit or restrict the Holy Spirit; it should comprise of time throughout the day. Allow Him to lead and guide you by offering graciously of your time. Submit to His yielding.

4.   Disperse from any negative speech or action and refrain from fruitless conversations, Proverbs 18:20-21 (AMP), "A man's [moral] self shall be filled with the fruit of his mouth; and with the consequence of his words he must be satisfied [whether good or evil]. Death and life are in the power of the tongue, and they who indulge in it shall eat the fruit of it [for death or life]."

5.   Don't consult with friends or family members; enter into counsel with your church pastor(s) or marriage counselor. (Proverbs 19:20, KJV tells us to "Hear counsel, and receive instruction, that thou mayest be wise in the latter end."

6.   Restore your relationship, your personal relationship, with the Lord. Exodus 34:14 warns, "For thou shalt worship no other god: for the Lord, whose name is Jealous, is a jealous God."

Table of Contents

Chapter 1

Let Me Be Blunt

"We cannot solve our problems with the same level of thinking that created them." Albert Einstein

＊＊

Before we partake on this journey, I want to change your pattern of thinking. Some of you looked at the list of things to commit to and thought *I don't have time for all of this* or *it don't take all that.* Some of you even went as far as to say, "Okay, I can follow steps 1, 2 and maybe 4, but I don't have time for 3 and this lady already said she's not a Pastor. Well, I am here to tell you to capture that thought! 2 Corinthians 10:5 (KJV) says, "Casting down imaginations, and every high thing that exalteth itself against the knowledge of God, and bringing into captivity every thought to the obedience of Christ." The enemy wants to capture your mind. He does not want you to fulfill your purpose and live as one. As Believers, it is important for us to operate in unity without any division, as a body of Christ and particularly in our marriages. 1 Corinthians 1:10 says, "Now I beseech you, brethren, by the name of our Lord Jesus Christ, that ye all speak the same thing, and that there be no divisions among you; but that ye be perfectly joined together in the same mind and in the same judgment." When you're not operating under the influence of the Holy Spirit, you have succumbed to the influence and suggestion of the enemy, and he has you where he wants you... divided and broken. I wrote this book to let you know I already thought about it. I already did it and I survived. My marriage survived and so can yours; it just takes your commitment to open yourself up, to be vulnerable, and to ask God to use you. First, know that your level of commitment is directly related to your level of success. I have watched couples see our journey and praise us for hanging on in spite of the times they told us we were crazy. I remember sitting where you are right now hoping God would give me the word to leave. I would sit in the bookstore looking for some encouragement. I read Stormie Ormartian's book *The Power of a Praying Wife*.[ii] I heard her testimony and thought, "Stormie, that's too much; I am not going to do all that." Fortunately, I had enough knowledge to see she had a wonderful marriage and whatever I called, "too much" or my favorite "overanalyzing the Word," she had a loving husband to come home to and I was in the pit of hell. Praises be to God because I said *I am up for the challenge*, if nothing else but to prove Stormie wrong. I knew that a large part of me wanted a divorce, but a small part of me wanted to make it work. I told myself God is not a God of confusion; His *yes* means yes and His *no's* mean no. I was not told *yes*. I had to decide that I was going to be obedient, as obedience is better than sacrifice and that's the Word. Written in 1 Samuel 15:22 (KJV): "And Samuel said, Hath the LORD as great delight in burnt offerings and sacrifices, as in obeying the voice of the LORD? Behold, to obey is better than sacrifice, and to hearken than the fat of rams."

I knew better than anyone a lesson learned would be repeated. I was once told by God to stay at a job I hated; I fought and struggled with the desire to quit. I remember going to work one Sunday, yes, I was working on Sundays. I had a conversation with one of the managers in another department who told me that my purpose there was not the position I held, but the ability to bring peace and calmness to the job, and that was a gift from the Holy Spirit. Knowing this didn't change my attitude about the job. I hated the job; it was taxing and stressful on my heart. I was working in the emergency room and on one particular day, there were three suicide attempts. In another room, a mother died and her son and husband were having an altercation. The EMTs could not assist until the police broke up the son and father. That woman's last vision was that of her son and husband fighting. Her son and his father had to be handcuffed to see her before she died. I hugged the teenage daughter, as she watched life pass from her mother and as she dealt with the anger she felt towards her brother and father. Across the hall, a young Asian woman found out she was pregnant and felt she shamed her family. The following day, a mother I knew was there because her daughter had attempted suicide, and she did not know why. I held her as she was contemplating what she had done wrong as a mother.

Over two nights, I saw full circle one mother lose a life while her daughter mourned and another mother crying at the thought of losing her daughter. I went to work the next day, a Sunday morning, and my first customer was a newly released convict that had served twenty years in prison; he had attempted suicide because he did not fit in anywhere. I held his hand, spoke words of encouragement, and left his room. I had a brief thought of my conversation with the manager just days earlier. That did not matter, because I was quitting the job and talking to God at the same time telling Him that I will deal with the consequences, but I had to go. I could not take another minute, another patient. I left my job and went to join my family at church. It was as if the entire family looked up at me unanimously, as if to say *you're not supposed to be here*. I felt like Jonah on the boat when the sailors came to throw him out to sea. I had the audacity to think that my disobeying God was right; after all, going to church would make it a little better and would somehow justify my leaving. Sunday services ended and I had to deal with my punishment. I thought of my mother and what she would say when we disobeyed her, "A hard head makes a soft behind." Well, my behind was soft. Hindsight is 20/20, but I recall in my study of this lesson a prayer asking God to help me, and give me strength to stay in the position.

Shortly after that prayer, the woman walked up to me at work and told me how valuable I was to the hospital. Now, you may ask how that story was helpful. My love language is *words of affirmation*, so He gave me what I needed. He impressed upon the heart of a manager to express gratitude in a way I would receive it. Lesson learned the hard way, but learned. I never left a job, church, or even released a friendship prior to the Lord telling me, because a lesson not learned will be repeated, and I learned my lesson. I share this story when people tell me that it's too much work.

Merriam-Webster defines *work* as any activity involving mental or physical effort done in order to achieve a purpose or result. I looked at my life and realized I did work to damage and we decided to do the work to repair it. We did the work, the mental and physical effort, to reap the benefit of wholeness, to reap the benefit of one flesh. I know my Lord is smiling at us both. So, I tell you trust what the Lord tells you and know that He will never leave you. Is it hard work? Yes. Is the reward great? Absolutely! You are leaving a legacy of a strong Christian faith, a wonderful relationship with your Heavenly Father, and a committed relationship to the man/woman of your youth. When you work on restoration, you will see the fruit you produce and it will be fruit of the Spirit, as discussed in Galatians 5:22-23 (KJV): "… love, joy, peace, longsuffering, gentleness, goodness, faith, meekness, temperance: against such there is no law." Praise the Lord! Now, I would like you to go back to the list of items to commit to (1-6) and allow God to move in your life.

Now, let me explain this book, *Dry Bones: God's Plan For Restoring Marriage: From Reconstruction to Restoration.* I share scriptures that were helpful in the restoration of my marriage. I typically use several versions of the Bible as a reference to highlight, or place emphasis on, the verse. The book is broken down into four sections. The sections are important in the process of reconstruction. In order to go through reconstruction, we must know where we came from to reprogram our thinking. Section one is the *Beginning.* I begin by telling you about our childhood; it's where we both find out how our weaknesses manifested themselves negatively in our marriage to take us on a path of self-destruction. Once this was identified, we could see the gateways that left us both very vulnerable to breakdown. Your story won't be ours, but as we share the information, along with insight, you will be able to see the pattern in your own life. I highly encourage you to journal; it is important to monitor your progress. Each section ends with questions to ponder. The questions are self-reflecting and designed to help you journal. This book is a direct reflection of me journaling my journey. I have learned to be strategic because you're at war and wars are won by being strategic in battle.

Section two is entitled *Self-Destruction*. We are very vulnerable, I more so than Darrick, because this book is based upon my journal. We share our trials and how loopholes were left open to bring about this destruction. Section three is based on our experience as we decided to repair our marriage. We call it *Road to Recovery*. This is our reconstruction! Reconstruction takes place as we reflect on past breakdowns, learned behavior from our childhood, and as we seek experts for guidance. Reconstruction is the process of building something that was damaged or destroyed, based upon Merriam-Webster. We accept that change is needed for recovery and restoration. Our counseling experience shares the good, bad, and a whole lot of ugly. We share how we thought maybe a civilized divorce would be the best option and even preparation for divorce helped us to continue counseling when we wanted to quit.

Section four is called *Reconstruction*. Our reconstruction is where we end counseling and walk in the healing presented to us; this is where we take ownership of our healing. We backslide and we fall, but He shows us how to get back on track. I believe it's here where you will learn the most. It's our recovery period as we learn to apply God's Word to our life. We recognize and take ownership of our responsibility to stay on the right path and how to recognize the signs, or *light bulb moments*. This is where we *recover all* as David did. Complete restoration! We conclude with tools and resources, I even include a journal entry from my personal journal. I pray you will have others to come to you and share how God is blessing them by seeing what He is doing in your life.

Remember, you're only a page away from your breakthrough. I don't mean that as a cliché; I am so confident that this book will bless your personal relationship with God and you will see the manifestation of God's love in your home and marriage. I believe wholeheartedly applying the tools that are offered in this book will restore your marriage. Not that this book or my writing has any power, but God's Word never returns to Him void. I say that because I am not a minister; I am a woman, wife, mother, sister, and daughter with no training in theology. I applied the Word to our lives. "So I prophesied as I was commanded. And as I prophesied, there was a sound, and behold, a rattling, and the bones came together, bone to its bone." Ezekiel 37:7 (ESV) Shall we begin? Hallelujah!

The Beginning

"The beginning is the most important part
of the work." ~Plato

Chapter $\mathcal{2}$

My First Classroom: Home

"Your kids watch you for a living. It's their job; it's what they do. That's why it's so important to try your best to be a good role model." James Lehman, MSW

My husband and I were raised in two very different households. I was the only girl of four children and yes, I was spoiled. My father died when I was four and my mother remarried. That remarriage was not before a few unsuccessful beaus. I was raised by my mother and stepfather. My mother handled all the finances, the order of the home, and the discipline of the children. My mother asserted ladies should be seen and not heard. However, she herself was boisterous, she was strong. Biblically, what I knew I learned by reading and having an innate desire for more. I learned that going to church was a requirement to enjoy other weekend outings. I never learned how to develop a relationship. We were sent to church and told by our parents to pray for them. Mom definitely ruled the roost in our home and fighting was witnessed often. Awakening to the yelling and cursing was the norm. Arguing was how they communicated. There was no order of respect. The order in our home was Mom, Dad, kids, and God. Now, God was only included during holidays and when my parents were dealing with some difficult times. My mother would play Gospel music in the home, but usually it was coupled with some sort of trouble or catastrophe. I associated God with someone to reach out to when I was going through. I missed the whole relationship with our Heavenly Father.

In spite of all the yelling and screaming, I was loved by my parents. I believed my mother and step-father gave me the best they could. My mother worked tirelessly trying to ensure we all had the latest and greatest everything. My stepfather supported me and my siblings as if we were his own children.

Light Bulb Moment!

First life lesson, or baggage, I learned to carry was manipulation, followed by avoidance of conflict and low self-esteem. I learned how to survive in chaos and disorder.

Everything I knew I learned from home. What a lesson I learned. I was growing up developing into a young lady. My mother had raised us to think that if we looked good, we felt good, and we always looked good. Four children, my mother did a fantastic job managing finances. The household income was supplemented by turning our home into a "shot-house". I was pouring drinks/shots for people before I turned "double digits," that would be ten-years-old. I would get loose change if the drink was filled to the rim; my second lesson on manipulation. I gave in easily to avoid conflict.

After all; these were grown men I had to pour drinks for and oftentimes, these men were already drunk. I don't know who turned our home into a "shot-house," but that's when home was no longer a safe haven. The older I became, the less safe I felt.

Light Bulb Moment!

Introduction to fear! Fear will play a major role well into adulthood.

I would kiss my parents goodnight and all the people who were in our home. I secretly hoped my mom would say no, so I would be saved of feeling like I was disrespecting the adults, but it became a part of the nightly routine. I hated it secretly but again, I was raised ladies are to be seen and not heard. I later learned at a young age, approximately eleven to twelve-years-old, that I was frisky. I didn't understand what *frisky* meant. My mother used to call me "frisk-pot," but for men to call me frisky, I knew it was something negative. I tried to get a sense of normalcy by reading books. I would walk a great distance to the library. I was isolated and not allowed much freedom, so the library was my escape and it awakened a passion in me. Whatever was going on at school or home, books were my escape, and I could be any character I was reading. This was my survival because over the course of the next few years, I went to some very dark places. Places that taught me I had no self-worth or value. I was invisible. Even now, I have to remind myself to be in the now, but it's not always easy to escape what's been your norm.

I was a people-pleaser. People who meant me no good, I had the desire to please. This carried over into every area of my life. I became whatever people needed me to be.

Light Bulb Moment!

I had no identity of my own and no self-worth. It is in the solitude of being in the presence of the Lord that we discover our purpose and our self-worth, it's not in people.

My mother became ill with MS (Multiple Sclerosis) when I was twelve-years-old. I became her caregiver very early. Doing everything to please her, I was already feeling like I was the adult, or the mother. I was the one child she thought would be perfect and here I was about to expose to the world that I was having premarital sex. By the age of seventeen, I was pregnant with my first daughter. I gave birth to my daughter when I was eighteen-years-old. My mother and father were furious to learn I was sexually active, let alone pregnant. We moved when I was seventeen-years-old and our new home was no longer stocked with top shelf. I did not have to pour drinks or live in fear of men under the influence in our home. That does not mean we did not have our own family nightmares.

Brittany was born and she was my anchor, my lifesaver. God had given me the opportunity to rewrite my story as her mother, not as Nycholle Woolfolk, but as Brittany's Mom. I had enough love for her to know that she would have a "better life". Not sure what it would be, but I clearly knew what it would not. I knew no men would touch her, because I had no trust with anyone. I knew she would be loved and feel love from the inside out. I would give her a loving home; she would be smart, intelligent, and articulate. Boy let me tell you, I got what I prayed for. She is articulate, intelligent, and beautiful inside and out. She is the epitome of a woman beyond her years.

Remember, what I thought of myself did not change because of Brittany. Those issues would surface later, because what you don't deal with will always have the ability to attack you later.

Chapter *3*

Darrick's First Classroom: Home

⌐ ⌐

My husband Darrick grew up with both father and mother. The eldest of five, Darrick's father died when he was sixteen-years-old, forcing him into adulthood/manhood early. Darrick's recollection of his father was protection and stability. Although his father was an alcoholic, he took care of the family. He was the head of his household and his mother took charge of the home. Communication was witnessed in yelling and arguing, as in my home. Although his mother and father argued, they presented a united front when disciplining the children. After the death of his father, he lost stability within the home and life forever changed. He was fortunate enough to have both maternal and paternal grandparents and a great-grandmother in his life. He was amongst so much wisdom. He is a living representation that it takes a village to raise a child. That wisdom would carry him through when he decided to marry a woman with children.

The passing of his father and soon after, his paternal grandfather would render him a fatherless young man at the early age of sixteen. It was a tragic car accident that left him with so many unanswered questions. Although his mother was strong, she had her own weaknesses when Darrick's father passed. As Darrick got older, he would take on the role as father to his younger siblings. However, when he felt "man-enough" to call-out his mother, she requested he leave. Darrick would make an attempt at college, but lack of financing left him with few options. Darrick was forced into joining the military. The decision to join the U.S.A.F. was a light at the end of a dark tunnel. That decision would give us the opportunity to meet.

Questions to Ponder

1. Reflect on your first classroom. Do you see obvious differences in the way you and your spouse were parented? List the differences.

_____

_____

_____

_____

_____

_____

2. Do you see evidence of how you were parented and the impact it continues to have in all areas of your life? Please consider your workplace, and home.

_____

_____

_____

_____

_____

_____

_____

3. I encourage you to find a scripture reference that speaks to the issue that has plagued you since childhood. Find a scripture and hold on tight to God's Word.

_____

_____

_____

_____

_____

_____

4. Why this scripture? When there's a *why* to the reason, you will own the scripture!

_____

_____

_____

_____

_____

_____

_____

_____

_____

_____

_____

_____

_____

Chapter 4

Our New Beginning As One

"Therefore shall a man leave his father and his mother, and
shall cleave unto his wife; and they shall be one flesh."
Genesis 2:24(KJV)

——— ✦ ✦ ———

Cleave means to adhere firmly and closely or loyalty and unwa-
veringly, according to Merriam Webster's dictionary online.
Darrick and I were required to go to counseling before our pastor
would agree to officiate the ceremony. Our counseling was good;
however, it was difficult to see beyond our current situation. We
had a strong relationship; Darrick wooed me and I wooed him.
We didn't have any of the issues our pastor discussed or made us
research. Darrick and I were both smitten with love. We finished
the counseling and scratched it off of our to-do list. We moved on
to more pressing things like picking out the meal, finalizing guest
list, and gifts for the bridesmaids and groomsmen.

Clearly, Darrick and I united without a firm foundation or understanding of what holy matrimony meant. The one thing we both
knew, he loved me and I loved him: wasn't love enough? No! We

both desired church and had a yearning to learn about the Lord. We went to church on Sundays together as a family and related to the messages, so that was enough, right? Wrong!

--- ➤ ◄ ---

Light Bulb Moment!

Don't let the routines of life stop your relationship with the Lord and each other.

--- ➤ ◄ ---

We both decided our children would be raised in church. We desired to give our children a personal relationship with the Lord, so Sundays we worshiped together as a family. Our first church home was that of a very close friend, Venee. She grew up in this church and her roots were deep. We all sat with her family on the second pew. The pastor, Reverend Bethel, married Darrick and I; and we began to grow roots. The women at this church nurtured me on how to grow into the woman my mother taught me to be. I watched as these strong women taught me, mentored me, on how to carry myself as a lady, a mother, and a wife; successful women, educators, administrators, professors, doctors, and attorneys. They gave me a standard, to pursue my education and raise my expectations for my children. This wonderful church, a church that embraced us as if we had always been members, was my foundation. Reverend Bethel was my first "spiritual father" and his wife, my "spiritual mother". Reverend Bethel died in 1998 and Venee passed away in 1999. No one knew the devastation this had on me. They were my measuring points, my compass, and my sounding board. Walking into that church without seeing either of them was devastating.

I was a stay-at-home Mom caring for my mother and four children. I was rather isolated. I had a few mothers in the neighborhood, but none like Venee. She was a born protector and would stay on Darrick. She would say the things to him that he could only receive from Venee. Our relationship began to suffer. Darrick would come home from work and expect to find the home free of any clutter and freshly vacuumed floors. He never openly expressed his disappointment; he would just start throwing toys in the proper place and would proceed to vacuum the floor. To me, this was hurtful because I never ran the streets or watched T.V. I was working trying to spend time educating and entertaining our children because money was tight. I would find great deals at yard sales and he would frown that it was junk. I began to hold on to the criticism and take things personally. I began to do things to please him and avoid conflict. I would fuss with the kids to pick up the toys, so everything was immaculate when he arrived. He would still walk in without a smile or a hello. I began to feel lonely and abandoned and with my friend gone, I was losing myself in pursuit of trying to find someone else's happiness.

Light Bulb Moment!

Stop trying to play God! You can't fill a hole that was not created by you, only God can fill that hole. Likewise, he could not fill my inadequacies. People-pleasers will try to fix-it.

Our issues were internal and they could only be fixed by God. My inadequacies manifested in the way he responded, or lack of response, when he came home. The fact is they were already there.

Darrick's issues were internal. My cleaning the house didn't make things better; his issues only manifested as a result of the clutter. There are things that only our Heavenly Father can help us with. Like Jesus said to the woman at the well, John 4:7-14 (KJV): "There cometh a woman of Samaria to draw water: Jesus saith unto her, Give me to drink. (For his disciples were gone away unto the city to buy meat.) Then saith the woman of Samaria unto him, How is it that thou, being a Jew, askest drink of me, which am a woman of Samaria? For the Jews have no dealings with the Samaritans. Jesus answered and said unto her, If thou knewest the gift of God, and who it is that saith to thee, Give me to drink; thou wouldest have asked of him, and he would have given thee living water. The woman saith unto him, Sir, thou hast nothing to draw with, and the well is deep: from whence then hast thou that living water? Art thou greater than our father Jacob, which gave us the well, and drank thereof himself, and his children, and his cattle? Jesus answered and said unto her, Whosoever drinketh of this water shall thirst again: But whosoever drinketh of the water that I shall give him shall never thirst; but the water that I shall give him shall be in him a well of water springing up into everlasting life. The woman saith unto him, Sir, give me this water, that I thirst not, neither come hither to draw."

We must understand that we are not put together to be one another's god, we have a God, a Heavenly Father. He wants us to be one, cleave to one another, and fill one another, but always put God first. He is the lover of our souls. Remember, we all have to deal with our own demons.

The kids came so quickly and before I knew it, I was a wife, a caregiver, and a mother, and I had no idea who Nycholle was.

Darrick felt as if he was a provider, just someone who worked and paid the bills. He was dealing with wanting more out of life and no matter how much I cleaned or vacuumed, it did not take away the burning desire to want more out of his life, out of his career. In my eyes, he was so much more, but it was in my eyes, not his. I believe Paul said it best in Philippians 4:11 (KJV), "Not that I speak in respect of want: for I have learned, in whatsoever state I am, therewith to be content." Learning to be content is not easy; we have grown accustomed to having things our way. Paul was preparing us, reminding us, that being Believers does not mean our days will always be glorious; some days we have to be content.

Questions to Ponder

1.   What is your definition of cleave? After looking deeper into the definition, do you believe you and your spouse have cleaved to one another?

_____

_____

_____

_____

_____

_____

2.   Where in your life do you need to stop playing God?

_____

_____

_____

_____

_____

_____

3. Do you realize why you have not allowed God to take control? Is there something from your childhood that influenced your decision to feel you need to control or fill the hole?

_____

_____

_____

_____

_____

_____

4. I encourage you to find a scripture reference that speaks to this concern. Find a scripture and hold on tight to God's Word.

_____

_____

_____

_____

_____

_____

5. Why this scripture? When there's a *why* to the reason, you will own the scripture!

_____

_____

_____

_____

_____

_____

Self-Destruction

"There are seeds of self-destruction in all of us that will bear only unhappiness if allowed to grow."
~Dorothea Brande

Chapter 5

The Wilderness

"Leave no [such] room or foothold for the devil [give no
opportunity to him]." Ephesians 4:27 (AMP)

———————— ✦ ✦ ————————

We found a new church home where we could lay roots. We
made the decision to join one Sunday and I believe it was the best
decision we could make for our family. We enjoyed the sound
Biblical teachings. It was refreshing to have a place to call home.
Later, Darrick began working two jobs and I was attending services
alone. We did have sessions where I read my notes to him. This
was our "fellowship time". Some Sundays, the message was so
defining I could not wait to leave service to stop by his 2nd job just
to tell him about the message. I had such a desire to study the
Word! I was learning and applying the messages to my life. I finally
had a spiritual mother and father again, and that was exciting. I
was going to church, applying the principals learned to daily life,
and anticipating the growth. I don't think there was a hungrier soul
in that sanctuary. As much as I was learning, no one told me I had
to gird up my loins, for the attacks of the enemy were about to
strike, and strike hard. Sometimes, a little knowledge can be
dangerous. I was attending services alone. I never had a neighbor

to turn to my left or right during service. I wanted desperately for Darrick to be there to share it with me. I needed and desired him to be there to my right and speak life in me, so that I could confidently turn to my left and know that I was speaking a word into the very soul of my man, my husband.

Light Bulb Moment!

Alone! This is a caution area; the feeling of loneliness would be the first attack of the enemy. Remember, he wants your mind.

The definition of *alone* according to Merriam-Webster is to have no one present. To go one step further, it defines *loneliness* as a feeling of bleakness or desolation. I was not alone nor was I lonely; I had an entire congregation worshiping with me. I had the Father, the Son, and the Holy Spirit in my presence. Don't let vocabulary or semantics define or label you. I allowed the enemy to get into my spirit. Remember, the attacks of the enemy are to influence your state of being. The enemy is there to discourage and destroy with subtle hints. Ephesians 6:10-18 (KJV) reads: "Finally, my brethren, be strong in the Lord, and in the power of his might. Put on the whole armor of God that ye may be able to stand against the wiles of the devil. For we wrestle not against flesh and blood, but against principalities, against powers, against the rulers of the darkness of this world, against spiritual wickedness in high places. Wherefore take unto you the whole armor of God that ye may be able to withstand in the evil day, and having done all, to stand. Stand therefore, having your loins girt about with truth, and having on the breastplate of righteousness; And your feet shod with the preparation of the gospel of peace; Above all, taking the shield of faith, wherewith ye shall be able to quench all the fiery darts of the wicked. And take the helmet of salvation, and the sword of the Spirit, which is the word of God: Praying always with all prayer and supplication in the Spirit, and watching thereunto with all perseverance and supplication for all saints."

In the beginning, things began to change dramatically for us, for the better. I started hearing and studying the Word more. I began to develop a personal relationship with the Lord. The Lord began blessing our family. I enjoyed our new church; however, I missed the fellowship and intimacy of my previous church. My mother was living with us and I was her caregiver. It was difficult to make new connections because so often, we would have to rush out of church to get home to my mother. Darrick was working some Sundays. Life was simple, we didn't have much, but we had each other.

I began to join a ministry at the church to meet people. Nursery ministry was my choice and I love children. When in service, I would sit in church most Sundays and Wednesdays alone. I remember when the pastor would say, "Turn to your neighbor." Most often, no one would turn to, what appeared to be, a single woman. No, the wives weren't having that, not even in the church. I would watch the men look their wives in the eyes and vice versa, repeating what our Bishop would say. I would stare in admiration because it would look as if they were speaking to each other's spirit man. It seemed to me that the couples were getting a double blessing. Sitting together, the husband's hand was stretched behind the wife's shoulder and the wife curled in the crease of his armpit. What a wonderful sight. That's something so powerful; you can't take that home and share. Darrick would attend church when he could, but he would be so involved in the message as the pastor would say turn to your neighbor, he would look straight ahead and just repeat what our Bishop requested. For me, this was devastating because I would look so forward to him being there and when he was there, it felt as if he wasn't. I felt more alone with him being right beside me than I did when I was alone.

♦ ◄

Light Bulb Moment!

We, as human beings, being flawed as we are, often have our spouses in competition they are not even aware exists.

♦ ◄

Darrick was in competition with the other members of our church and he had no idea. He didn't know what I was seeing every Sunday when he could not attend. The more he came, the more I envied his presence, as it was worse. There is no loneliness like the loneliness you feel when you have someone right there with you. I was giving a foothold to the devil. At least alone I had no one to direct anger towards, but to have him beside me and not with me, I was lonely and I had someone to project that anger onto. The enemy didn't allow me to see that I should delight in my husband worshipping the Lord and focus on our Bishop's teaching. I was so focused on what my husband wasn't doing with me, instead of what he was doing with the Lord. He was in a state of worship and it had nothing to do with me, it wasn't about me. I should have been rejoicing, thanking our Father for placing a spirit in him to desire to hear what the Lord had to say. It never dawned on me that my husband was in love with the changes God was making in my life, he wanted to taste it. He saw the God in me and he, too, wanted to know that God, at the level I knew Him. I was in competition with the Lord, and there's no competition there, the Lord will win and you, as I, will lose. I was allowing the enemy to block my blessing, our family's blessing.

✦ ✦

Light Bulb Moment!

Oh no, enemy present; envy and bitterness. The enemy is here to kill, steal, and destroy. Maya Angelo gives a good description of envy and bitterness, likening it to a cancer that eats upon the host.

✦ ✦

The enemies of envy and bitterness were finding comfort with me and in my home like a cancer. I began to challenge my husband and he was always very angry and bitter. He began to argue with the kids and me daily. He was harsher in his discipline towards the kids and I felt the need to be more lax to compensate, or balance, the discipline. I no longer believed everything he said and with the computer at hand, I could prove him wrong. Big mistake! This only opened the door to another demon: disobedience, the demon came in and I invited him. Romans 5:19(KJV) says, "For as by one man's disobedience many were made sinners; so by the obedience of one shall many be made righteous." I challenged him in front of the children, "You don't know what you're talking about, that's not right" or the old time favorite, "I will prove you wrong". The children were watching. Our Bible time changed because now we were contaminating the Bible study sessions. I was curtailing the message to suit my point. Highlighting or putting emphasis where there was none, contaminating God's Holy Word. We were going to church and I was tapping his foot and he was tapping mine. Wow, looking back, we were both stupid. The kids were starting to get involved: "Mom, that's you." Or overtly laughing and nudging. Matthew 12:33 (KJV) states: "Either make the tree good and his fruit good; or else make the tree corrupt, and his fruit corrupt; for the tree is known by his fruit." Church had begun to play the reverse role in our lives by tearing down the message or each other. We were the only family leaving church beat down, instead of lifted up.

Light Bulb Moment!

Don't use God's Word or fellowship times as a platform to validate your viewpoint, because God does not need your help!

The true Word of God will minister to the person it needs to at the time He wants the message to be delivered. Sometimes, the very message ministered to you will be what God is showing you He is going to do in your life, not your spouse's. Sidebar for a moment: I have a good friend and she's always telling me about the Word and how it relates to the many flaws she sees in her husband. I am a transformed woman with a made up mind, so when people share with me the flaws they see in their spouses, I simply say this, "Pray for your spouse." If you spend more time in prayer and less time in finding Scripture to focus on their flaws, God will reveal to you, more often than not, that it's you standing in the need of prayer. I don't believe in fighting with Scripture; I believe Scripture is there to help us grow and the Holy Spirit gives us discernment to show the love of Christ and demonstrate that love to one another. I don't care how perfect you are; you will always find ways to improve yourself. Matthew 7:3-5 says, "Why do you stare from without at the very small particle that is in your brother's eye but do not become aware of and consider the beam of timber that is in your own eye? Or how can you say to your brother, Let me get the tiny particle out of your eye, when there is the beam of timber in your own eye? You hypocrite, first get the beam of timber out of your own eye, and then you will see clearly to take the tiny particle out of your brother's eye." End of sidebar.

⟶ ⟵

Light Bulb Moment!

New enemy: division.

⟶ ⟵

Romans 16:17-18 (KJV) says, "Now I beseech you, brethren mark them which cause divisions and offenses contrary to the doctrine which ye have learned: and avoid them. For they that are such serve not our Lord Jesus Christ, but their own belly; and by good words and fair speeches deceive the hearts of the simple." However, The Message Bible reads: "One final word of counsel, friends. Keep a sharp eye out for those who take bits and pieces of the teaching that you learned and then use them to make trouble. Give these people a wide berth. They have no intention of living for our Master Christ. They're only in this for what they can get out of it, and aren't above using pious sweet talk to dupe unsuspecting innocents." Winston Churchill said, "When there is no enemy within, the enemies outside cannot hurt you." Division builds a wedge; in our case, a gap was forming. I hope your ears are open to hear and eyes open to see that the enemy comes to steal, kill, and destroy.

Please understand these weren't overt attacks against my husband, they were subtle. This is how the enemy works; we didn't wake up one day and say alright, today I am going to use everything I have in my possession to destroy you. No, it was subtle a discussion here, a debate there, and escalation after escalation. Matthew 12:25 (KJV) states: "And Jesus knew their thoughts, and said unto them, Every Kingdom divided against itself is brought to desolation; and every city or hose divided against himself; how shall then his kingdom stand?"

Light Bulb Moment!

New enemy: rebellion.

When church is no longer a place of solitude, you begin to look outside for consolation. My prayer and worship time was under attack, because now I did not feel clean or worthy to approach the throne. I turned my focus to education and work. Wanting gratification that was instant, whether by graded paper or promotion. My attire changed, as I was looking for the immediate attention a little makeup and sexy clothes offered. I went from frugal shopper looking for traditional style clothing that would not go out of style to the faddish tops and bottoms that were in and out with the seasons. The current minivan did not fit the profile of this new "woman" I was becoming.

Light Bulb Moment!

I had new tastes and new desires, a new enemy: the Jezebel spirit. A very manipulative spirit, controlled by lust and seduction.

Ephesians 2:2 (AMP) says, "In which at one time you walked [habitually]. You were following the course and fashion of this world [were under the sway of the tendency of this present age], following the prince of the power of the air. [You were obedient to and under the control of] the [demon] spirit that still constantly works in the sons of disobedience [the careless, the rebellious, and the unbelieving, who go against the purposes of God]." I would place bets on how many drinks I could get someone to buy me. To look that good cost me a pretty penny, not just financially, but spiritually. I was the center of attention wherever I went and I loved it. It didn't matter to me that I had not paid my bills, because I just spent $150.00 or more on a cute little outfit. I was paying my husband back for all the years he did not appreciate my sacrifice, the frugality of a virtuous woman. He could handle the bills because it would look bad on him if we did not have electricity or water, right? After all, he is the "head of the household" the "King of the castle". *Pay the price buddy* was the attitude I had.

Light Bulb Moment!
New enemy: devour!

1 Peter 5:8 (NIV) states: "Be alert and of sober mind. Your enemy the devil prowls around like a roaring lion looking for someone to devour." Tithing was not being fulfilled; especially, since we were missing service. Money was going in and out of my hands like it was water. I had new desires that came with a price tag. I had always been very cost conscious and frugal, but I began to see frugality as an enemy. Money was to be spent and not saved. I was more interested in building relationships with the retailers, than my husband. At home, I was criticized and chastised. At the store, I was welcomed, admired, and appreciated. Stores would hold new items in the back, because they knew I would be in to look over it and purchase. I was shopping, eating out, and spending like I had a money tree. Now, my excuse was that I was a great Mom and I deserved to have fun. I would take care of home with cooking and cleaning, but *after hours* on certain nights was reserved for me to have fun. The more Darrick criticized and complained, the more others appreciated me, or so I thought. Devour was creeping up on me and it was new to us, as we had never been in debt. Does any of this sound familiar? I am sure it does.

Light Bulb Moment!
New enemy: deception!

I need to clarify; in my mind, at that time, it felt as if I was taking care of home. I was taking care of the cleanliness of the house and basic care of the children, but I was ignoring my home and the needs of my children. Cooking, cleaning, and providing care is not taking care of the home. I was not setting a Godly example of a wife or a mother. I was not demonstrating the Proverbs 31 or Titus 2 woman. Proverbs 31:10-31 (KJV) says, "Who can find a virtuous woman? For her price is far above rubies. The heart of her husband doth safely trust in her, so that he shall have no need of spoil. She will do him good and not evil all the days of her life. She seeketh wool, and flax, and worketh willingly with her hands. She is like the merchants' ships; she bringeth her food from afar. She riseth also while it is yet night, and giveth meat to her household and a portion to her maidens. She considereth a field, and buyeth it: with the fruit of her hands she planteth a vineyard. She girdeth her loins with strength, and strengtheneth her arms. She perceiveth that her merchandise is good: her candle goeth not out by night. She layeth her hands to the spindle, and her hands hold the distaff. She stretcheth out her hand to the poor; yea, she reacheth forth her hands to the needy. She is not afraid of the snow for her household: for all her household are clothed with scarlet. She maketh herself coverings of tapestry; her clothing is silk and purple. Her husband is known in the gates, when he sitteth among the elders of the land. She maketh fine linen, and selleth it; and delivereth girdles unto the merchant. Strength and honour are her clothing; and she shall rejoice in time to come. She openeth her mouth with wisdom; and in her tongue is the law of kindness. She looketh well to the ways of her household, and eateth not the bread of idleness. Her children arise up, and call her blessed; her husband also, and he praiseth her. Many daughters have done virtuously, but thou excellest them all. Favour is deceitful, and beauty is vain: but a woman that feareth the LORD, she shall be praised. Give her of the fruit of her hands; and let her own works praise her in the gates."

Meditate on the verses of a virtuous woman; know that we may not be all that is listed in the 21 verses right now, but we should aspire to be as close to a virtuous woman, as possible.

I know I have listed a lot of evil spirits. I would like you to note that I called them out; I noticed what I was working against. I did not gain this insight and understanding overnight. I learned this later by journaling and spending time in the presence of the Lord. I want you to understand that journaling the good, the bad, and the ugly reveals a lot to you. As the Scripture Romans 16:17 (KJV) states: "Now I beseech you, brethren mark them which cause division and offense contrary to the doctrine which ye have learned; and avoid them." To mark them is also writing them, journaling them.

I could go on and on and list every demon, as I am now very wise of his attacks; this book would have another title. I just wanted you to see how easy it is to allow yourself to open a portal for the enemy to gain access. I am not trying to scare you, but it is true there are a heaven and a hell. There is a portal where the enemy, if you give him access, will come in and attack you. Key word, you have to give him *access*. This is real. It is so important for you to protect your portals. When I mention spirits, or enemies, I think of fruits of the flesh, as in Galatians 5:19-21 (KJV). "Now the works of the flesh are manifest, which are these; Adultery, fornication, uncleanness, lasciviousness, idolatry, witchcraft, hatred, variance, emulations, wrath, strife, seditions, heresies, Envyings, murders, drunkenness, revellings, and such like: of the which I tell you before, as I have also told you in time past, that they which do such things shall not inherit the kingdom of God. But the fruit of the Spirit is love, joy, peace, longsuffering, gentleness, goodness, faith, meekness, temperance: against such there is no law." What are you producing the Fruit of the Spirit or fruit of the Flesh? I urge you to carefully review the fruit in your life. My examples have all resulted from fruit of the flesh: wrath, strife, and envy.

We all produce fruit; we just have to understand our actions, whether positive or negative, will produce fruit, and consciously decide to produce the Fruit of the Spirit. I have learned to watch my actions so that I always walk in the Fruit of the Spirit. Once we become aware of the power of our actions, we are able to control our actions, thus controlling whether we're operating in the Spirit or the flesh. Before I respond in any discussion, I think of the response and ask myself which fruit am I sowing? It's easier to teach your children when you're modeling self-control and responding with the Fruit of the Spirit. To take a deeper look at what God says about our fruit, let's look at the Message version of Galatians 5:19-24. "It is obvious what kind of life develops out of trying to get your own way all the time: repetitive, loveless, cheap sex; a stinking accumulation of mental and emotional garbage; frenzied and joyless grabs for happiness; trinket gods; magic show religion; paranoid loneliness; cutthroat competition; all-consuming-yet-never-satisfied wants; a brutal temper; an impotence to love or be loved; divided homes and divided lives; small-minded and lopsided pursuits; the vicious habit of depersonalizing everyone into a rival; uncontrolled and uncontrollable addictions; ugly parodies of community. I could go on. This isn't the first time I have warned you, you know. If you use your freedom this way, you will not inherit God's Kingdom. But what happens when we live God's way? He brings gifts into our lives, much the same way that fruit appears in orchard-things like affection for others, exuberance about life, serenity. We develop a willingness to stick with things, a sense of compassion in the heart, and a conviction that a basic holiness permeates things and people. We find ourselves involved in loyal commitments, not needing to force our way of life, able to marshal and direct our energies wisely." Now, I can't state it any clearer than the unadulterated Word of God.

As women we're delicate, fragile creatures designed to be a helpmate for our spouse. When we do anything contrary to the task of being a helpmate then we are working against God's original intention for us. We know that God created man and later woman; however, Yandian[iii] shares this analogy, "It was more than a rib God took out of Adam; He pulled out the spirit and soul of Eve. He used the rib to manufacture her body, but her spirit already existed, having been created when God created Adam's spirit." When you learn that your spirit was created before you were born, it was pulled from your husband, your helpmate.

Thinking of this, is it even possible to live in discourse? Yandian further gives an analogy of Jesus and the Church, "The way that God made Adam and Eve, took Eve out of Adam, and then brought her back to him is a type of Jesus and the Church." When I read this, it spoke volumes to me because in Genesis 1:27 (KJV) it says, "So God created man in His own image, in the image of God created He him; male and female created he them." In Genesis 2:7 (KJV) it states: "And the Lord God formed man of the dust of the ground, and breathed into his nostrils the breath of life; and man became a living soul." However, when the Lord created woman, He did not breathe life into her because she, we, came from life, the life of our husbands. Genesis 2:21-22 (KJV) says, "And the Lord God caused a deep sleep to fall upon Adam, and he slept: and he took one of his ribs, and closed up the flesh instead thereof; And the rib, which the Lord God had taken from man, made he a woman, and brought her unto the man." It's important to know whose we are and who we are. I was created to cleave to my husband and anything contrary to that is contrary to my make up as a woman, and will only produce fruit of the flesh, which ultimately leads to death. My desire is to show how strong God is and not to glorify the devil. Ephesians 3:19 (AMP) says, "[That you may really come] to know [practically, through experience for yourselves] the love of Christ, which far surpasses mere knowledge [without experience]; that you may be filled [through all your being] unto all the fullness of God [may have the richest measure of the divine Presence, and become a body wholly filled and flooded with God Himself]!"

Gary Chapman wrote a book entitled *The 5 Love Languages*[iv]. In this book, he does an in depth study of the way we receive love or how we connect. The 5 Love Languages are: Words of Affirmation, Acts of Service, Receiving Gifts, Quality Time, and Physical Touch. It's an awesome book that shares how to love our spouses in a way they can receive our love. In looking over the five types of love languages, you may think you have one dominant love language, until you read the book. I learned I have multiple love languages, my most dominate is quality time and acts of service. Most people love the way they receive love and this book is a testament that's not successful.

Questions to Ponder

1. List words that you realized you have used inappropriately? List them and bring them under subjection of the Word of God. I.e. Loneliness/ I am never alone for Jesus left me a Comforter who is with me every day. Proverbs18:24... there is a friend that sticketh closer than a brother.

_____

_____

_____

_____

_____

2. To what or whom do you have your spouse in competition with?

_____

_____

_____

_____

_____

3. Are you operating in the Fruit of the Spirit or fruit of the Flesh? Find ways that you can model the Fruit of the Spirit, list them.

_____

_____

_____

_____

_____

_____

_____

4. I have listed a few demons that plagued me; what demons do you find present at this point in your reading?

_____

_____

_____

_____

_____

5. I encourage you to find a scripture reference that speaks to this concern. Find a scripture and hold on tight to God's Word.

_____

_____

_____

_____

_____

6. Why this scripture? When there's a *why* to the reason, you will own the scripture!

_____

_____

_____

_____

Chapter 6

I've Fallen, I Can't Get Up

> "Humble yourselves [feeling very insignificant] in the presence of the Lord, and He will exalt you [He will lift you up and make your lives significant]." James 4:10 (AMP)

I was rebelling in every aspect of our relationship. What I felt I could control, I did; whether intimacy, or time. I knew the things I could and could not control and it made me feel powerful. Key word here *power*. As I stated in *My First Classroom-Home*, I was the only girl. I knew enough about the Word to know what I was doing was wrong and yet I could not reel myself back. A new improved Nycholle was forming and she even scared me. I was wearing so many hats and so many different personalities: the church lady that cursed her husband getting out of the car, the dutiful mother who made sure kids were well respected serving on every committee and volunteered to help on every project, the knowledgeable daughter who knew more than any nurse or doctor, in most cases, and the girl who could light a club up with her presence. Boy, did Satan have me deceived. I could put on a show. I knew I was wrong; I knew my life was a lie, but I didn't know how to stop and every time I thought about changing, Darrick would do something else to make me angry.

———— ✦ ✦ ————

Light Bulb Moment!

Did you see that? Darrick would do something to make me angry.

———— ✦ ✦ ————

Ecclesiastes 7:9(KJV) says, "Be not hasty in thy spirit to be angry: for anger resteth in the bosom of fools."

We were both puppets and we allowed distractions to take us off course. Distractions are designed to do just that, take us off the path God has provided us; I had fallen and I couldn't get up. Fallen, pounded by distraction, and a rebellious spirit. I could see the division in my children. I was walking in the fruit of the flesh and I could not see my way out. Galatians 5:19-21 (KJV) says, "Now the works of the flesh are manifest, which are these; Adultery, fornication, uncleanness, lasciviousness, Idolatry, witchcraft, hatred, variance, emulations, wrath, strife, seditions, heresies, Envyings, murders, drunkenness, revellings, and such like: of the which I tell you before, as I have also told you in time past, that they which do such things shall not inherit the kingdom of God."

They were walking in the fruit of the flesh and it was our fault. All four children were rebelling in one way or another. They were living what they were learning. I would apologize daily to the kids for me and their father's behavior. I was living a direct contradiction to what I was teaching, and we know children learn what they live. I had fallen and I could not get up!

--- ➤ ◄ ---

Light Bulb Moment!

Prayer was not working because the enemy knows the Word and will take it out of context in an attempt to corrupt you; he did the same to Jesus.

--- ➤ ◄ ---

The enemy works diligently to break your connection from the Lord when you allow sin in your life. He attempts to sever the relationship between you and the Holy Spirit, and it's typically done by condemnation. Don't let the enemy win!

Matthew 4:6-7 (KJV) states: "And saith unto him, if thou be the Son of God, cast thyself down: for it is written, He shall give his angels charge concerning thee: and in thy hands they shall bear thee up, lest at any time though dash thy foot against a stone. Jesus said unto him, it is written again, Thou shalt not tempt the Lord they God." Jesus realized who He was. Every time I would kneel down to pray, I would hear the enemy tell me, "Only the prayers of the righteous availeth much, and you're not righteous." I would hear the enemy tell me, "A just man falleth seven times and you have fallen more than seven times today. How can you be forgiven, you're not just." Boy, I was being worked overtime, and I did not know how to respond; I did not know how to be forgiven! Embarrassment and shame overwhelmed me. I wanted help, I wanted resolve, and I wanted forgiveness, but I didn't know where to go! Death seemed the only option, so I prayed for death. I prayed for my life to come to an end. I had fallen; fallen so deep into sin, I could not get up! 1Peter 5:8 (KJV) says, "Be sober, be vigilant;

because your adversary the devil, as a roaring lion, walketh about, seeking whom he may devour." I welcomed it. I felt I deserved it.

If this sounds familiar, please pray and ask God to come into your heart, forgive you for your sins, acknowledge in the presence of the Holy Spirit what you have done, and ask for His forgiveness. Ask Him to create a clean heart and renew a right spirit within you. Sing songs and hymns unto the Lord. Mix up lyrics from songs that you know; it's not about you, it's about Him. Let Him know He and only He is the lover of your soul. Pray and sing songs of praise if you don't know where to begin. Say JESUS three times out loud and the Holy Spirit will be moved and take over. Cry out to Him as if your life depends upon it, because it does; your soul depends upon it. Start there, that's where I started; I cried out to God. I asked Him to take away the sin, the lust, the deceit, the anger, the bitterness, and to change my stony heart to a heart of flesh. My prayer, it was me, me oh Lord, standing in the need of prayer! I cried out to My God as if my very life depended upon it, because it did and does; your very life depends upon it, too.

I began to get up and at that very moment, I made the decision to restore my relationship with the Lord. It was not about Darrick or the kids; it was about me and my relationship with my Heavenly Father, the first lover of my soul. For the first time, I released, I let go, and I let myself be naked before the Lord. I allowed Him to be in control. I can honestly say it felt good, to truly let go and give it all to Him. I had to acknowledge my Father's grace and mercy. My situation was so big! I had messed up royally and if I had never taken another breath, I wanted to go out worshipping Him, my Heavenly Father. I was broken! This was the first time I was so tuned into the Lord. I could not hear the enemy, and he could not come in this space, for it was holy ground. Have you ever truly surrendered all to God? Have you ever been in His presence? It is impossible to be in the presence of the Lord and not be changed, forever. When you are in the presence of the Lord, there's no doubt, fear, thoughts of being unworthy, or rejected. To be in the presence of the Holy One, you don't try to make excuses, you simply fall to your face in forgiveness and humility, as you are wrapped in His love. It's beyond amazing! It was in that very moment that I learned to cast all my cares upon Him for I was broken.

Psalm 51 (KJV) is a passionate prayer David prayed to God after the Prophet Nathan reminded him of his sin. I refer to this prayer often, because it's a reminder that God does forgive us of our sins. Remember, David sinned and fell short, but he is regarded as a man after God's own heart. "Have mercy upon me, O God, according to thy loving kindness: according unto the multitude of thy tender mercies blot out my transgressions. Wash me thoroughly from mine iniquity, and cleanse me from my sin. For I acknowledge my transgressions: and my sin is ever before me. Against thee, thee only, have I sinned, and done this evil in thy sight: that thou mightest be justified when thou speakest, and be clear when thou judgest. Behold, I was shapen in iniquity; and in sin did my mother conceive me. Behold, thou desirest truth in the inward parts: and in the hidden part thou shalt make me to know wisdom. Purge me with hyssop, and I shall be clean: wash me, and I shall be whiter than snow. Make me to hear joy and gladness; that the bones which thou hast broken may rejoice. Hide thy face from my sins, and blot out all mine iniquities. Create in me a clean heart, O God; and renew a right spirit within me. Cast me not away from thy presence; and take not thy holy spirit from me. Restore unto me the joy of thy salvation; and uphold me with thy free spirit. Then will I teach transgressors thy ways; and sinners shall be converted unto thee. Deliver me from blood guiltiness, O God, thou God of my salvation: and my tongue shall sing aloud of thy righteousness. O Lord, open thou my lips; and my mouth shall shew forth thy praise. For thou desirest not sacrifice; else would I give it: thou delightest not in burnt offering. The sacrifices of God are a broken spirit: a broken and a contrite heart, O God, thou wilt not despise. Do good in thy good pleasure unto Zion: build thou the walls of Jerusalem. Then shalt thou be pleased with the sacrifices of righteousness, with burnt offering and whole burnt offering: then shall they offer bullocks upon thine altar."

Do you know what it means to be naked before the Lord? I think of Adam and Eve, after eating the fruit of knowledge, they were ashamed and they hid in shame, because their nakedness exposed the sin. Well, to be naked before the Lord in this form of worship is letting God know you recognize His Sovereignty and that your sin is shameful, and you know He and only He can wash away your sin. *Naked* is defined by Merriam-Webster as without clothes. You often see naked used to describe food or a drink that has no preservatives or additives. I am speaking of *naked* as being conscious and willingly exposing ourselves to God. He who already knows everything about us because Jeremiah 1:5 (KJV) tells us: "Before I formed thee in the belly I knew thee; and before thou camest forth out of the womb I sanctified thee, and I ordained thee a prophet unto the nations."

We come before the Lord in prayer and sometimes we summarize or minimize our actions, as if He won't pick up on what we've done. To be naked before the Lord, as I am describing, is an act of submitting before the Lord, our sins and shortcomings, and asking for His love, His forgiveness, and His grace, all of which we are unworthy of. Nakedness is knowing we're unworthy and yet believing, as we surrender all, He is just to forgive us. The act of surrendering means we recognize the fleshly, worldly influences on our lives and openly break that influence. You're a broken individual, naked before a Sovereign God who desires to pick us up and put us back together again, but not as before. No, we're stronger this time because the cracks and crevices known as *scars* by the world become our testimony, our armor to lift others up. We are no longer defined by worldly attributes, our looks, net worth, or material gain.

We have an infinite strength, access to an Omnipotent, Omnipresent God who will never leave us or forsake us. I was exposed standing before my Creator, not having to say what I have done because He knew. I was ashamed and I fell to my knees as a little child rocking back and forth wanting to be consoled, yet I was worshipping Him. Scriptures were rolling off of my tongue that I did not know I had committed to memory and I hadn't, it was the Holy Spirit. At that very moment, I knew I was forgiven. He held me like I was a child, like a father would hold his little girl, and I was that little girl. Luke 18:16-17 (AMP) says, "But Jesus called them [the parents] to Him, saying, Allow the little children to come to Me, and do not hinder them, for to such [as these] belongs the kingdom of God. Truly I say to you, whoever does not accept and receive and welcome the kingdom of God like a little child [does] shall not in any way enter it [at all]."

I am not describing my experience to you in anticipation that your experience will be likened to mine; no, I am sharing this with you as a guide to show how I experienced brokenness. Once I experienced brokenness in its true unadulterated form, I knew there was a God and He never left me. He was there through all my pain; He just needed me to call on Him. I think of a baby taking his first steps. As parents, we want to help him, we stand there in great anticipation waiting ready to embrace or soften the fall, but we understand if they are ever going to walk, they have to do it alone and when they fall, we are right there to help. I believed my Father was there to experience my fall and there to pick me up when I called out to Him. He is a part of me, He lives in me, and once you experience the power of His love, you truly understand who you are and Whose you are; it becomes easier to accept forgiveness and extend forgiveness.

For our time here is temporary and once we get perspective, we are able to change. You must understand that you can't walk in condemnation. There is no condemnation in Christ Jesus for Romans 8:1 states: "There is therefore now no condemnation to them which are in Christ Jesus, who walk not after the flesh, but after the Spirit." We are also reminded in John 12:47: "And if any man hear my words, and believe not, I judge him not: for I came not to judge the world, but to save the world." Condemnation comes from the enemy not from God. Condemnation will tear you down and leave you feeling alone and desolate. Condemnation is what caused me to pray for death.

Questions to Ponder

1. I believe we all have redefining moments or times when the *light bulb* comes on. Comedians even add it in the act joking that if the light bulb doesn't come on, check the bulb. Well, as you have read the previous chapters, is there any defining moments that have caused you to pause or say *ah-ha?*

_____

_____

_____

_____

_____

_____

2. Have you recognized times you have dug your heels in the ground refusing to budge? No one wins when you dig your heels in. Write it down and surrender it to the Lord. He alone is able to relieve your burden; all you have to do is surrender to Him. Are you ready to surrender to Him?

_____

_____

_____

_____

_____

_____

3. I described in the best way possible my experience surrendering to the Lord. I want you to describe to the best of your ability your sweet surrender to our Heavenly Father. Capture in words how you released all your cares to Him. If you accepted the

Lord as your personal Savior, I want you to write the experience. If the Lord reveals anything to you, write it down. Remember, God is a Holy God who loves you and wants to be in control, allow Him!

_____

_____

_____

_____

_____

_____

_____

_____

_____

_____

_____

_____

_____

_____

_____

_____

_____

_____

_____

_____

_____

_____

Road to Recovery

"There is one consolation in being sick; and that is the possibility that you may recover to a better state than you were ever before." ~Henry David Thoreau

Chapter 7

Seeking "Godly" Counsel

"So I say to you, Ask and keep on asking and it shall be
given you; seek and keep on seeking and you shall find; knock
and keep on knocking and the door shall be opened to you."
Luke 11:9 (AMP)

→ ←

I was reading at the bookstore when I stumbled across a friend
I had not seen in years. I had been thankful to God for the work
He was doing with me, but the enemy was still very much present
in my home. I had been in prayer about finding an outlet where I
could remove the desire to drive by old spots I had visited in the
past. I had been praying for the Lord to give me a Godly place to
be on Tuesday nights. The meeting of this friend on Tuesday was
no accident; it was an answer to my prayer. I will call it a *divine
appointment*. She invited me to a woman's fellowship group on
Tuesday night's and she offered to pick me up. I was so excited!

+ +

Light Bulb Moment!

God is our refuge and strength, a very present help in trouble. (Psalm 46:1) Cast your cares to Him and you will see the scriptures begin to come to life.

+ +

God provides us with our hearts desires; we just have to ask and have a heart to receive. During the meeting, I realized Darrick and I both needed Godly counseling with someone who had survived the hurt our marriage had suffered. Darrick and I had been through counseling in the secular realm and in our church; however, neither one of us was willing to fully divulge all our issues; after all, our pastors were perfect and had never experienced the hurt that we had. We could not come before them fully naked and unashamed. In the secular realm, the counselors approved of divorce, but I never felt content. The counselors felt our marriage could not survive and felt that divorce would be the best option. Both of us felt our family was worth more than simply throwing in the towel. Hindsight is 20/20, but I truly believe we didn't go along with the divorce, because we both knew in our hearts we weren't being completely honest. Our words and our actions spoke divorce, but in the pit of our bellies, we were not at peace with that resolution.

The ladies group I was attending on Tuesday night was facilitated by a wonderful woman who happened to be a pastor's wife. Look at God, strategically positioning this meeting. No one could have planned this divine appointment but God. After several weeks of attending this group and hearing the testimony of the other ladies, I was able to share my story without fear of judgment. I learned the pastors, themselves, had survived hurt and betrayal. They were willing to share their testimony. She shared my story with her husband and he was willing to counsel us, as long as we had permission from our home church. Our church has an awesome Bishop and first lady that represent what a Godly marriage is made of; however, we needed to see someone who had survived betrayal, and abuse.

We went to see our Pastors and asked if we could enter into counseling with this pastor at another church, as we needed to see someone who had been through the fire and came out as gold. We knew the importance of doing things in decency and in order. 1 Corinthians 14:40 (AMP) says, "But all things should be done with regard to decency and propriety and in an orderly fashion." Our Pastors released us to enter into counsel with another church and I thank God. Our Pastors understood our needs and the desire to rebuild our marriage, and did not confine us to our home church. They graciously blessed us to seek counsel and keep them informed of our progress. We could never have received the breakthrough without the blessing of our pastors. We are forever grateful.

In a day when church members are hopping from one church to another, they did not feel the need to hold on to us; they allowed us to be under their teaching and be counseled by another without feeling threatened. The counseling, once a week, was followed by a women's fellowship with the pastor's wife and men's fellowship with the pastor. This went on for several weeks, even months before breakthrough. The men's and women's fellowships were called Life Groups. These Life Group sessions were essential to our healing. They allowed us to be open and vulnerable in front of our sisters and brothers and when I didn't have strength to hold on. Hearing their breakthrough testimonies gave us the encouragement and strength to hold on. When we felt our marriage couldn't take it anymore, they were able to stand in the gap for us.

I recall once sharing something Darrick was doing in my ladies group that I did not tell my pastor during a counseling session. This information was shared with my counselor and we were able to address it the next week. Our counselors were more concerned with our total healing, than our own personal feelings. I was grateful the information was shared and addressed. This is how counseling, at its best, works. It exposes the hurt by pulling up the root. Pulling up the roots will oftentimes expose new hurt, but it's necessary for complete healing and forgiveness.

> ⟡ ⟡

Light Bulb Moment!

When you're seeking true healing, don't expect overnight success.

> ⟡ ⟡

Set reasonable expectations. It did not take our marriage a month or a year for division to come in, so it will take more than one month to restore. You must focus on the end result; pay attention to the journey, the healing that takes place along the way. We had to trust God and be naked before counselors, friends, prayer partners, and each other. It was not easy; it was very difficult. It takes four years to earn a degree, another two to four for Masters and beyond. Even then you have to continue your education with continuing education courses or certifications. In a marriage you say, "I do" and it's done. You may receive premarital counseling; unfortunately, there is nothing in place that states you have to get certified, or even continue your counseling for prevention. Yet, a failing marriage is devastating to God, the individuals, the children, family members, and the many young couples that are watching you. Please know that you are being watched by couples who are looking at you to see how you maintain your relationships, household, and lifestyle. Live life like someone's watching. Remember, God is always watching.

I want to discuss preparing for marriage. It is important to prepare. *Prepare* is defined as to put in proper condition or readiness. To prepare you must put forth action. When you take two individuals and they decide to marry to become one, this process is bigger than the wedding ceremony and responding *I Do's*; it's the initial process of preparing to become one flesh. A part of preparing for marriage is seeking godly counsel, as you are taking two individual people and making one. Taking two individual people and making them think as one is a difficult task when you don't have God at the center. Our culture does not teach us to think in terms of two people uniting as one. This concept goes against our very grain. It is not possible for you to go to the store if your legs won't allow you to get up and move, well one flesh means that. It means doing what appeals to the other because the other is a part of you, you are the other. Recognizing that you say *no* to yourself to please the other; for example, if my husband said I don't want you to buy the car right now, I don't think we can afford it. This means I have consulted with my spouse and although I feel I can afford it, I will not buy the car. You have to recognize that someone leads and the other follows. Let's stay here a moment with leading.

There are many definitions of lead; however, Merriam-Webster's definition clearly agrees with how I am using the word *lead*. *Lead* is defined as to guide on a way especially by going in advance; to direct on a course or in a direction; to serve as a channel for. Business News Daily polled 15 Great Entrepreneurs[v]; Tom Kennedy defines leadership as getting people to want to follow. That requires engaging them passionately, from the heart, and requires persuading people to change. Ephesians 5:21-33 (KJV) says, "Submitting yourselves one to another in the fear of God. Wives, submit yourselves unto your own husbands, as unto the Lord. For the husband is the head of the wife, even as Christ is the head of the church: and he is the Saviour of the body. Therefore as the church is subject unto Christ, so let the wives be to their own husbands in everything. Husbands, love your wives, even as Christ also loved the church, and gave himself for it; That he might sanctify and cleanse it with the washing of water by the word, That he might present it to himself a glorious church, not having spot, or wrinkle, or any such thing; but that it should be holy and without blemish. So ought men to love their wives as their own bodies. He that loveth his wife loveth himself. For no man ever yet hated his own flesh; but nourisheth and cherisheth it, even as the Lord the church: For we are members of his body, of his flesh, and of his bones. For this cause shall a man leave his father and mother, and shall be joined unto his wife, and they two shall be one flesh. This is a great mystery: but I speak concerning Christ and the church. Nevertheless let every one of you in particular so love his wife even as himself; and the wife see that she reverence her husband."

God wants us to submit to one another. *Submit* is defined as to give over or yield to the power of authority of another. When we submit to one another in the fear of God, we understand that we submit to the will of the Lord. The husband leads based on the Word. The Word says the husband is the head of the wife. The husband is the head because he has the responsibility to love us as Christ loved the church and gave His life for the church. When I think of the love Jesus has for each of us, I believe that is the order God intended for marriages.

Now men, when you are king of your castle, you don't have to shout it on the rooftops. Jesus didn't walk around shouting titles or His birthright. He led with love and a servant spirit. The passage first states we submit to one another. When we cleave to one another, we are submitting to one another. Leading means there is one at the head and by him being at the head, he does not abuse, neglect, or discredit the other's value or worth. Leadership recognizes each other's strengths and weakness and uses them effectively in a partnership. I am much stronger in areas than he is and I never stand out and say this is my forte, but with grace, he understands and takes my advice. We have a healthy balance of who we are and the role we play as husband and wife. We are to lift one another up and encourage one another. There is no way for one to go up and leave the other behind. If you are growing and increasing, so should your spouse. When you begin to look at your marriage and recognize that you are not living your marriage the way God intended, then you read, meditate, and pray. A good place to start is Ephesians 5:21-33.

Seeking Godly counsel begins with knowing where you are and where you came from. There's an old saying *hindsight is 20/20* and it's true. When you have gone through and are on the side of healing and restoration, you see clearly the error of your way. I am often asked what advice I could give people before marriage to make sure they make the best choice in a mate. Well, I share a story that I believe is great life counseling 101. It stems from a conversation I had with a very good friend. We were discussing selecting a car and how much care I placed on picking out my dream car. I had been looking for a vehicle, being mindful of the questions to ask and what to look for in terms of pricing. I had gathered all the information that my husband was going to ask me, he likes when I do my homework. I had been toying with the idea of purchasing a new car and I am very frugal; I had looked for over two years now. I wanted a Mercedes S class. I have been in prayer for some time; however, I typically joke and say, "Suze Orman, financial guru, does not believe I can afford one, so I keep putting it off." Well, I visit the dealership and that suppresses the desire, temporarily. I have done the research, checked the reviews, looked at maintenance costs, and if you asked me anything about the car, I know all the facts. I was driving home after my salesman called me in to look at a used S Class, without the car I might add. I left the dealership and was talking to my girlfriend discussing how we spend more time and research on selecting a vehicle, than in the selection of a mate. I put a little chart together for review. Here are my notes:

Car	Spouse
We get the car facts, reviews, and opinions of other owners.	We don't get the facts about the person or counseling. You don't stop to ask important questions.

Anticipate trouble w/in 5 yrs. or more and estimate the cost of repairs and maintenance.	We think we can change them if they don't do what we say, we don't calculate the work or effort.
Research the manufacturer's warranty and consider the benefits of the extended warranty.	We don't do initial investigation to ward off potential long-term problems. We don't look at the family's relationship or marriage perspective on divorce, or rearing of children. Financial habits in terms of spending and saving?
Purchase with thoughts of how long before replacing.	We think if it doesn't work, we can replace.
How many miles will we get?	Lease with option of marriage.
Finally, we negotiate.	We don't compromise, our way or the highway.

When I share that story and the line by line comparison, it always seems to makes them think. I love to get your juices flowing and mind working. I know we should not look at marriage as a purchase of a car, but oftentimes, I listen to people who purchased a car and say, "Yeah, I did my research." However, they get a man or woman and it's the physical appearance, the finances, or the car they drive, but no one ever says they looked under the hood. Mr. or Ms. Right may look like they got it together, but what was their foundation? What is their view on working it out, how easily did they give up on previous relationships? These are the questions you need to ask? When my children were growing up, I would ask them about their friend's parents and that would determine the type of relationship they would have. If my daughter has a friend who is being raised by a single parent and she has a different boyfriend every week, the play dates will be held in my home. If my son has a friend that has both parents in the home and they drink in the presence of the child, then play dates are held in my home. I watch carefully the sphere of influence in my children's lives. If you raise them anticipating greatness and being watchful of the home environment; when they are older, they will know how to look at families of potential spouses. They are mindful of relationships between parents and their friends, and they look for inconsistencies.

Chapter 8

The Biggest Lie Ever Told

"Fill up and complete my joy by living in harmony and being of the same mind and one in purpose, having the same love,
being in full accord and of one harmonious mind and intention."
Philippians 2:2

❧ ❦

The biggest lie ever told is a simple mathematical equation
where half of anything combined with another half will equal a
whole. Many of us believe that we can meet in the middle; I will
take one step and you take another but in reality, you can't meet in
the middle. If you give 50% effort and your spouse gives 50%
effort, you will get half the effort. You will never make a whole
marriage. In any line of work or business if you provide 50% effort
to the task at hand, you will be terminated. If you are to become
one flesh, you have to be whole and your partner has to be whole,
and you both have to give one hundred percent, or one whole.
When you become one, as in one flesh, there is no such thing as
putting in half. If you have ever seen the movie *Not Easily Broken*[vi]
by T.D. Jakes, he speaks of the three strands; a cord of three
strands is not easily broken. Ecclesiastics 4:12 (KJV) says, "And if
one prevail against him, two shall withstand him; and a threefold

cord is not quickly broken." The three strands are husband, wife, and God. The three-strand cord is a braid of the marriage union that God intertwines together, so you don't see one without the other; you're unable to separate one strand of the cord without severing the connection of the remaining two braids. A braided cord is strong and it is not easily broken. It is intertwined dependent of one another. Is that not the relationship you want to have? A three braided cord, a solid union of husband, wife, and our Heavenly Father. One that is not able to be infiltrated.

A braided cord can hold a boat safely at pier when wind gusts and tidal waves are pulling against it. Understand, we are not fighting against tidal waves; this three-stranded cord is able to withstand the attacks of the enemy. We must understand the power of God in our union. God desires for us to live as one. When you have grown accustomed to giving fifty percent, the concept is hard to understand. When you don't understand the importance of God being in the center of your marriage, at the head of each of your lives, you make yourself susceptible to the enemy. Understand you must give 100%; anything less than giving your whole will always leave your marriage in a mediocre state, susceptible to infiltration. We serve a God that wants to multiply our marriage, our union, and our blessings.

Light Bulb Moment!

When you gain understanding that God works in multiplication and not in addition, you will open the doors to so many blessings.

Be very clear that when your mind understands and accepts this concept, you begin to think whole. God does not compute in simple math; He works in complex equations and formulas to multiply us.

One multiplied by one is one, and our union is God's multiplication. When you were joined together, it was to multiply. God commands Noah in Genesis 9:1 (KJV), "And God blessed Noah and his sons, and said unto them, Be fruitful, and multiply, and replenish the earth." Genesis 9:7 (KJV) states: "And you, be ye fruitful, and multiply; bring forth abundantly in the earth, and multiply therein."

Think in terms of offering all you have. When paying a bill instead of saying I am going to pay half, say I have this amount to contribute to this bill, what do you have? Another example, I am going to treat him to a pedicure without thinking of when the last time he treated me to a pedicure, and vice versa. Stop thinking your way out of something. Stop calculating if it's worth it, or if it's reciprocated. If God lays upon your heart to treat your spouse to something, don't you let your mind overthink it by calculating incorrect equations taught and demonstrated since elementary school? This is your man/woman and you can't deprive yourself of something. Luke 6:31 says: "And just as you want men to do to you, you also do to them likewise." Once you fully understand this concept and practice it, your whole world will change for the best!

Chapter *9*

The Journey

"Can two walk together unless they agree?" Amos 3:3

—————————— ✦ ✦ ——————————

Our counseling was hard work! The minister who counseled us believed in accountability. We had counseling every Tuesday evening. The sessions began and ended in prayer. We heard the testimonies of others and shared scriptures that guided and strengthened us. We were given examples of God moving and restoring lives. All sessions required active participation. Our counselor challenged us to read God's Word and pray for one another. We were never judged. The Tuesday sessions were wonderful because if I was hurting, we did not have to go home together to sulk, so I would leave counseling and go to fellowship, which strengthened me. Darrick would be left home to prepare the kids for the next day and sulk. Some Tuesday nights, I would purposely go home late to prevent arguments about our counseling sessions. I was so thankful for the full days that prevented us from arguing.

Light Bulb Moment!

Avoidance is never good; it leaves no room for healing.

Even though, for me, avoidance was great because I am not confrontational, Darrick, however, likes to debate and discuss. In so many ways, I was preventing him from healing with my avoidance. This is actually another level of control. By avoiding confrontation, it did not allow us put into practice the techniques we learned in counseling. I had to share this with my counselor and learned this was abusing control, and changes would have to be made. My Life Group did not end; I just came home early to allow discussions in a healthy format.

The numerous counseling sessions opened up wounds that I thought were closed and there were times divorce seemed inevitable. We moved from hating one another to understanding we loved each other; we just could not live together. Our counselor suggested going on an encounter, an *Encounter* is a retreat where you go and encounter the Lord. You take only a blank notebook, a Bible, your clothing, and toiletries. You are purposely paired with people you don't know. We both went through an encounter; not only was this encounter needed, it allowed us to see who we were. I received my breakthrough in an encounter where I received the Holy Spirit, and my prayer language. I had to recognize that I had to be truthful and not have a lying tongue, and it was at that moment that I received the power to speak in tongues. *Encounter* was not about Darrick and I, it was about perspective, and I needed perspective, because at the time of *Encounter*, we were still contemplating a respectful divorce. Encounter was about me and the Lord! Getting closer to the Lord, to hear His voice and be obedient. I got more from the experience than I ever anticipated.

Boy, oh boy! I remember coming to grips with my molestation that I had been carrying around for years. I remember the Lord wrapping His arms around me and letting me know sex is more than an act. I had been married for over ten years and had never seen sex as making love and for a long time, I could not say the words. I coupled the sexy clothes at a party and men gawking with sex. The awful act that lasted minutes, but was forever on my mind, forever left for me to carry a burden. *Encounter* allowed me to hear what God had been speaking to me for a long time, "Come here Tamar, you're a tree! You are strong, and I love you. I have always been there, wrapping My arms around you, now scream, baby scream, and let it out! Let all the hurt and pain go."

I did, I kicked and screamed as if my life depended upon it, and with every scream, I felt purged, refreshed, and renewed. My Encounter with the Lord is where I got my life back. That's where I learned how to trust the Lord. If He was there at my worst, as a child, He was still there. He loved me in the midst of my sin and shame; He loved me. I continued in fellowship after *Encounter* and then started attending a prayer group. I wanted to learn how to use my prayer language and how to pray, not just talk to the Lord, but pray. I was in a time of prayer when God spoke to me and asked if I wanted Darrick to go to heaven or hell. I didn't understand, but in prayer, I learned it was not about me, it was about God. It was about Darrick and I being one, of one flesh! I could not grow and leave Darrick behind, it was my job to allow God to show Himself strong through me. I had to die to self, as Peter says, *die daily* because it is not about me, it's about winning a soul to Christ and allowing ourselves to be used by God. How can you truly be a fisher for the souls of men and leave yourself behind?

> <

Light Bulb Moment!

Marriage is a ministry.

> <

Don't forget the Great Commission! Ultimately as Believers, we want our spouses and children to be saved, and it starts in our home.

1 Corinthians 15:31 says, "I affirm, brethren, by the boasting in you which I have in Christ Jesus our Lord, I die daily." This was truly a moment where the *light bulb* went off. I realized that it was not about me. I was happy with my relationship with the Lord; however, it was so much bigger than me. I was winning souls for the Lord and it was not going to be easy. Every time I would feel like giving up, someone would walk over to me and compliment how great we looked together. People would tell me how they admired how much my husband adored me. Those comments allowed me to see the bigger picture. People are looking at us and people were assigned to us, they needed to see the Lord work in us so that they could get through, just as my counselors had been there for us. I got it and it strengthened me.

Chapter *10*

Working It Out Yourself
(Find a Scripture and Hold On For Dear Life!)

"And he said unto me, My grace is sufficient for thee: for my strength is made perfect in weakness. Most gladly therefore will I rather glory in my infirmities, that the power of Christ may rest upon me." 2 Corinthians 12:9 (KJV)

❖ ❖

The ultimate goal of counseling is taking what you have learned and being able to apply it to daily life. Our counseling sessions came to an end. After counseling, I eventually stopped going to the Woman's Life Group. This was a difficult decision, but there are times when you get dependent upon the counselors and not on God. God showed us that we needed to be in His presence. Alone time with Him; my Heavenly Father needed me to cry on His shoulders and ask Him for guidance. When you are walking with God and obeying, He will tell you when it's time to let go.

Light Bulb Moment!

When God removes someone out of your life, it's never to sub-tract from you. Remember, God multiples, He does not subtract.

He will remove only to place you in the right space of mind to bless you. He wanted to ground us in His Word to bless and multiply our union. The Bible, His Word, became our confidant and counselor. If I felt Darrick was mean, I would say he was wonderful and he loved me. If I felt he did not appreciate me, then I would speak Colossians 3:23 (KJV): "And whatsoever ye do, do it heartily, as to the Lord, and not unto men." Also, Romans 4:17(KJV) which says, "(As it is written, I have made thee a father of many nations,) before him whom he believed, even God, who quickeneth the dead, and calleth those things which be not as though they were." I found a scripture that I held on to in the midst of everything! Romans 8:28(KJV) states: "And we know that all things work together for good to them that love God, to them who are called according to his purpose." When I needed to be intimate, I prayed to God that He would give me desire, desire I had lost because I was still harboring un-forgiveness. Un-forgiveness is powerful and it is not of God. When you are dealing with un-forgiveness, you cannot move; you're stagnating, which is just where the enemy wants you.

I studied often Darrick's love language, his needs versus my needs and how they conflict. I needed to realize that my feelings were under attack. As the serpent and Eve in the Garden of Eden, I was being used in my marriage. My feelings were impacting my relationship, and I had to understand it for what it was. I began to study my Bible and recognize the attacks of the enemy. I began to apply the Word to my life and I began to speak God's Word. I found conflict was less likely to arise and I began to truly grow. I closed loop-holes and prayed for anointing. This was not a story book healing; boy, I would still fall and backslide! The difference now was I knew I had my Heavenly Father next to me encouraging me. He was the Rock I leaned on. His love was far greater than any emotion the enemy attempted to use to distract me. I wanted to please Him and my faith was strong; I believed I would get out of my marriage what I put into it. I bombarded myself with Gospel television, classes on managing a Godly home, and marriage classes. I ended friendships and relationships with people who spoke negatively in my life.

This may sound a little uneasy for most people, but if you have a best friend that fills a gap that should only be filled by your spouse, then you have to let it go, because it's out of order with the plan of God.

<hr>

Light Bulb Moment!

No one should be a closer friend to you than your spouse.

<hr>

If you have a best girlfriend or best guy friend or partner that you consider your *ride or die chick/dude* or even a child, there is a problem. If you are truly committed to the "relationship" with your spouse, then you should evaluate your priorities. Your best friend (that ride or die friend) should be your spouse, period. My best friend held a higher place in my life; she was my confidant and when things were rough for her, I was there and vice versa. However, this is not the divine order. We are still very good friends, but if my husband needs me, then he takes precedence. My husband is now my best friend. I realize I respect his feelings more when I don't have someone else taking his place. Trust me, initially, you will miss the relationship with your friend; however, you gain so much more. I still have my girl's night out, but only when it does not conflict with my husband's needs. I will tell my friends *no* in a heartbeat now, which is something I would not have done previously.

✦ ✦

Light Bulb Moment!

Remember, God is a God of order.

✦ ✦

You don't realize how out of order you are until you start getting in order, or aligned with the Word of God. Once you take the first step towards order, you are acknowledging the value God places on order, thus making room for Him to guide you into a more perfect order in every area of your life. I remember God speaking to my heart one day and He asked me to pray for my husband the way that I pray for our children. Wow, this was big because I use to say the *one liner* for my husband, but go into an elaborate prayer for the children praying a hedge of protection, praying for their future wives or husbands, praying for their friends, and calling out their names before the Lord each and every day and night. My husband needed that prayer and I realized just how much I neglected him. He has such authority and position and

I did not think he needed me to pray for him like I prayed for our children.

＞ ＜

Light Bulb Moment!

Pay attention to your prayers, they will tell you about the order of your home and life.

＞ ＜

My house was out of order and it was the subtle changes I made that made the most difference in our relationship. You won't know the subtle changes that need to be made, unless you listen to the still voice of the Lord. He will reveal at each level of growth your mate needs. I began to truly listen to his troubles at work and pray for him, his job, and anyone in his sphere of influence. I began to pray for his day, over his body, and I began to see what his place was in our home. I began to see the things he did for our family. When you're out of order, the enemy will let you believe lies and hide from your heart the blessing you have. I did not think my husband was a protector. I had forgotten the small things he would do when we went out to dinner how he watches over us, if we attend a buffet; we all get our plates first, as he watches over the table and us. He is always looking to assure protection over our family. I made light of this when I should have appreciated it. He ensures doors are locked, cars are inspected, and we have cash in case of an emergency. Every night, he ensures my cell phone and Bluetooth are charged. He looks out for our family's wellbeing. I used to get upset when he would ask me when is my next scheduled mammogram or Pap smear, and following through to ensure I didn't forget to schedule them.

I am not writing this because I want you to add this to the list of things your spouse does not do; I want you to think of the small things they do. If it's washing your car, watering a plant you love, or starting the coffee pot in the morning because he knows you love coffee, let's appreciate our spouses. Men, if your woman assesses your wardrobe to make sure your tie matches or you have clean socks, appreciate her for the little things. Let us not take one another for granted.

I must talk to the wives for one moment here because we must manage our time wisely. As helpmates, we have a full plate, but we're able to do all God has placed before us. The key is organization. We must listen to the Lord. It means uninterrupted time seeking the Lord in silence allowing Him to order our days. You have to train yourself to listen to the Lord, because we're so accustomed to listening to family members and friends and were trained to be auditory, but we have to retrain ourselves to listen to our hearts. As a wife and mother, we wear so many hats, when you add work outside the home, care of elderly parents, and extra-curricular sports and or activities, this just adds to your already busy schedule. God grants us all grace as Believers. Whatever He has tasked us with; He has provided us grace we need to complete it without pulling from our first ministry, our home. I love Merriam-Webster's definition of *grace*: unmerited divine assistance given to humans for their regeneration or sanctification. It is wonderful to know that my divine right is grace and that I am entitled to it as a Believer. He provided me with regeneration and sanctification. When I think of regeneration, that is a revival, or rebirth, and sanctification. It also says it is the state of growing in divine grace as a result of Christian commitment. He already knew we would get tired, overwhelmed, and stressed but He, being all knowing and all powerful, provided us with grace to sustain us. Hallelujah! Give Him glory!

I typically write down a list of things I need to accomplish for the month, week, day, and hour. I have a planner that includes a monthly at a glance, weekly date planner, daily planner with hourly timeslots, and it includes a *to do* list. I use this every day to help keep me focused on completing tasks. As women, we need to have a plan of action. Benjamin Franklin has been credited with saying "if you fail to plan, you plan to fail." I believe it's directly related to the scripture Habakkuk 2:2 which says, "And the LORD answered me, and said, Write the vision, and make it plain upon tables, that he may run that readeth it." There is something to writing out your vision.

Our Heavenly Father wants us to be happy and successful. He has set us up for success. We have to pray and ask God to lead us. I find that when I value the hours and minutes of my day, He multiplies my time. It is as if I get up from prayer, whether it's been thirty minutes or an hour, and the time stood still. When I worked a "job-job" and told people all the things I had accomplished before my work day, they did not believe me. God says in Malachi 3:8 (KJV), "And I will rebuke the devourer for your sakes, and he shall not destroy the fruits of your ground; neither shall your vine cast her fruit before the time in the field, saith the LORD of hosts." The Lord wants to restore and multiply our time. Anything we do for our God is considered profitable use of time and when you make profitable use of time, your time is blessed. We have to make sure that this time is used to honor God.

We see this as Martha complains to Jesus that Mary was not helping. Martha, the server, wanted to serve Jesus; she was concerned with making sure Jesus and His disciples were comfortable as in Luke 10:40-42 (KJV). "But Martha was cumbered about much serving, and came to him, and said, Lord, dost thou not care that my sister hath left me to serve alone? Bid her therefore that she help me. And Jesus answered and said unto her, Martha, Martha, thou art careful and troubled about many things: But one thing is needful: and Mary hath chosen that good part, which shall not be taken away from her." As you can see, Jesus told Martha, as we have to tell ourselves, we're so busy on the serving piece, we forget who we serve. Can you imagine sitting at the feet of Jesus, the One who fed the multitude with two fishes and five loaves of bread as told in Luke 9? I hope I would see the joy in sitting at His feet versus ensuring the others were fed. After all, He is the Messiah, in the flesh; I would hope that I would have the good common sense to kneel at His feet to learn and hold on to every word He uttered. We are Martha's every day we decide if the housework or entertaining friends is more important than sitting with our Lord in prayer waiting for a Rhema Word.

Men, I have to also address that working it out yourself means you have to spend that quality time with the Holy Spirit, so you're able to minister and cover your wives. Darrick would express some dissatisfaction with me on a particular issue and I would ask him to speak to the Lord about it. Trust the process because if God is the cord that binds you together, He is the cord that keeps you together. Don't go to a friend to share what your wife is not doing or another woman; go to your Father. I don't know why people are comfortable praying to the Lord for a job, a car, or increase in wealth, but won't go to the Father for the changes they need from their spouses. Psalm 37:4 (KJV) says, "Delight thyself also in the LORD; and he shall give thee the desires of thine heart." If you desire to have your wife iron your clothes before work, or cook dinner; anything you're looking for your wife to do instead of arguing, take it to the Lord in prayer. Don't get discouraged once you prayed; the Lord will reveal to you what you need to do to receive those desires. Typically, the more you pray about your wife/husband, the more God will reveal to you your own missed opportunities.

Remember, we're no longer thinking in terms of meeting in the middle, we're thinking in terms of the whole. Change your mind set and you will change the outcome. Think of it this way, if you change what you put in, ultimately, you will change what you get back. If you put in your head the Living Word of God, you will get back a wife/husband that will want to serve you because God will reveal what is missing in your spouse, in an effort to answer your prayer. I find the more I would pray to God about how I wanted Darrick to be, the more I learned how much I needed to change. The more I changed and served like God told me, the more Darrick changed. We were both happier, because we ultimately worked on ourselves.

Chapter 11

Enough is Enough

"We are hard-pressed on every side, yet not crushed; we are perplexed, but not in despair; Persecuted, but not forsaken; cast down, but not destroyed." 2 Corinthians 4:8-9(NKJV)

Our struggles did not end because we decided to recommit ourselves to one another, no; the true attacks came as we got closer to the Word. We continued to have some very basic struggles with communication, rearing of our children, and respect for one another. Don't think that once you make the decision to serve the Lord and unite your marriage that you won't be tested. The Bible states in Luke 11:25-26 (AMP): "And when it arrives, it finds [the place] swept and put in order and furnished and decorated. And it goes and brings other spirits, seven [of them], more evil than itself, and they enter in, settle down, and dwell there; and the last state of that person is worse than the first."

There has been so much division that trust was very hard. Habits began to form and Satan was constantly looking for an opening. I would bump into people who had not seen me in a while and they would state, "You're divorced now, aren't you?" Proverbs 16:1 (NIV) states: "To man belongs the plans of the heart, but from the Lord comes the reply of the tongue." No one, not even Christians, believed we were still together.

— ✦ ✦ —

Light Bulb Moment!

Please don't put your trust in man, because they will fail you.

— ✦ ✦ —

Trust the plans of the Lord and He will reveal and make very clear the plan for your marriage. If you're to stay together, He will reveal it to you and give you the grace needed to heal the marriage. Don't think that Christians will all rally in support of you staying together and working it out. Oh no! Some of the very people I thought would be praying for us were actually hopeful that we let go. Stand on the Word of God, trust only the Lord, and if He says to stay, trust me, He will restore the time lost in quarrels. For our God is a restorer! Psalm 30 (KJV) says: "I WILL extol You, O Lord, for You have lifted me up and have not let my foes rejoice over me. O Lord my God, I cried to You and You have healed me. O Lord, You have brought my life up from Sheol (the place of the dead); You have kept me alive, that I should not go down to the pit (the grave). Sing to the Lord, O you saints of His, and give thanks at the remembrance of His holy name. For His anger is but for a moment, but His favor is for a lifetime or in His favor is life. Weeping may endure for a night, but joy comes in the morning. As for me, in my prosperity I said, I shall never be moved. By Your favor, O Lord, You have established me as a strong mountain; You hid Your face, and I was troubled. I cried to You, O Lord, and to the Lord I made supplication. What profit is there in my blood, when I go down to the pit (the grave)? Will the dust praise You?

Will it declare Your truth and faithfulness to men? O Hear, O Lord, have mercy and be gracious to me! O Lord, be my helper! You have turned my mourning into dancing for me; You have put off my sackcloth and girded me with gladness, To the end that my tongue and my heart and everything glorious within me may sing praise to You and not be silent. O Lord my God, I will give thanks to You forever."

It was hard to stay encouraged day in and day out. I began journaling. The journaling helped to show progress, progress that was measurable. This was enough encouragement to help me through the difficult days because my growth was evident. I would look at what I journaled a week earlier and I saw the progress and realized the journey was not so far out of reach. I held on to this progress, the promise that God would restore my marriage, our marriage. We began to grow, but there were distractions, our children. Our children were challenging us in so many directions. The children were not satisfied with the change because over the past couple of years, we were so divided they had learned to play the two of us. Now all of a sudden, as it appeared to them, it was a little too late. As we were building a stronger bond recognizing that we were one, the kids were playing us. They simply needed our guidance, direction, and more importantly, our united force. I kept thinking about how tired I was of fighting. I was tired of fighting to save my marriage and didn't feel I had the energy to fight to save my children, as they were doing exactly what we taught them. We created the situation and we had to be diligent enough to clean it up.

I read a book once entitled, *All I Really Need to Know I Learned in Kindergarten*[vii]. I remembered the title was enough to help me to realize that I needed to take the rest of the time I had with my children to teach my girls how to be a wife and mother and teach my boys what to look for when selecting a wife. I had my work cut out, but I was determined because my first ministry is my home. I began to see the defiance I was showing my husband in the kids and the anger my husband was showing me was being displayed among the kids. *Children Learn What They Live*[viii] was a poem written by Dorothy Law Nolte,

> If children live with criticism, they learn to condemn.
> If children live with hostility, they learn to fight.
> If children live with fear, they learn to be apprehensive.
> If children live with pity, they learn to feel sorry for themselves.
> If children live with ridicule, they learn to feel shy.
> If children live with jealousy, they learn to feel envy.
> If children live with shame, they learn to feel guilty.
> If children live with encouragement, they learn confidence.
> If children live with tolerance, they learn patience.
> If children live with praise, they learn appreciation.
> If children live with acceptance, they learn to love.
> If children live with approval, they learn to like themselves.
> If children live with recognition, they learn it is good to have a goal.
> If children live with sharing, they learn generosity.
> If children live with honesty, they learn truthfulness.
> If children live with fairness, they learn justice.
> If children live with kindness and consideration, they learn respect.
> If children live with security, they learn to have faith in themselves and in those about them.

If children live with friendliness, they learn the world is a nice place in which to live.

The human body and mind is resilient. This poem exemplifies how our children learn what they live. Parents, we have a responsibility to give our children the best possible start in life. We must teach them how to live. Many of Darrick and my flaws were a result of what we lived. I did not want my children to struggle; I wanted them to have a full life of love and happiness and most importantly, develop a real relationship with the Lord.

I mentioned early in the book to put on the whole armor of God, based on the Scripture Ephesians 6:10-18 (KJV). Bible scholars discuss the Scripture is based on the roman soldier in preparation for battle. As a soldier prepares for battle, they armour themselves in gear designed to prevent injury and ultimately save the soldier's life, while defeating the enemy. Each garment is likened to that of a spiritual battle where we're guarding our minds, hearts, and our homes. Let me explain, I would often hear "Girl, you must put on the whole armor of God." No one ever explained how the "whole armor" was put into real life terms.

Paul was writing to Ephesus, he was preparing them, the church for the many attacks they were about to face. We're never told to fight; we're instructed to simply armor ourselves with the whole armor, girdle of truth, breastplate of righteousness, shoes of readiness, shield of faith, helmet of salvation, sword of the Word, and prayer. Each piece of armor is vital in ensuring one's safety. Since we're not properly taught to stand in preparation for the attacks of the enemy, we respond via the flesh and attack. The battle is first because we wrestle in the Spirit, not in the flesh. Our battles are made manifest in the flesh, because we don't pay enough attention to passages10-13. When I look at the scripture, the passage introduces its first armor in passage 14; the more powerful passages in the Armor of God are passages 10-13. "Finally, my brethren, be strong in the Lord, and in the power of his might. Put on the whole armor of God, that ye may be able to stand against the wiles of the devil. For we wrestle not against flesh and blood, but against principalities, against powers, against the rulers of the darkness of this world, against spiritual wickedness in high places. Wherefore take unto you the whole armor of God, that ye may be able to withstand in the evil day, and having done all, to stand."

God wants us to be strong in Him, not in our own might. He wants to be big in our life. We are not to rely on our own strength to fight because in our own might we see flesh, but God sees the Spirit. In Matthew 16:22-23 (KJV) it says, "Then Peter took him, and began to rebuke him, saying, Be it far from thee, Lord: this shall not be unto thee. But he turned, and said unto Peter, Get thee behind me, Satan: thou art an offence unto me: for thou savourest not the things that be of God, but those that be of men." Jesus knew that Peter was not talking, it was Satan. Jesus addressed Satan with His love for Peter still intact. In our own might, we attack the person (flesh and blood) and not Satan (principalities, powers, rulers of the darkness of this world). God is preparing us for what is known. When you have full understanding of verses 10-13, you are able to go into the armor. One of the more powerful pieces of the armor is not physically described in verse 18: "Praying always with all prayer and supplication in the Spirit, and watching thereunto with all perseverance and supplication for all saints."

We have to recognize the power of prayer. We must pray in the Spirit with all prayer and supplication in the Spirit and watching thereunto with all perseverance and supplication for all saints. Supplication is defined as to ask earnestly and humbly. We must recognize that we have a sovereign God that has the ability to change the heart of any person. How dare we think we are more superior to Him who is the Alpha and the Omega, praise and Glory to God!

Questions to Ponder

1. Define your understanding of One Flesh, how has it differed?_____

_____

_____

_____

_____

_____

2. Pray and ask God to reveal to you ways you can consciously give 100% to your spouse. What has the Holy Spirit revealed to you? This may take a moment: think of what came to mind as you read our story; it may be as simple as starting up the coffee pot for your spouse.

_____

_____

_____

_____

_____

3. God demands that we do everything in decency and in order, with that being said, who are you praying for? Are you willing to assess your prayer life to get your house in order? What has God revealed to you about your prayer life?

4. I encourage you to find a scripture reference that speaks to this concern. Find a scripture and hold on tight to God's Word.

5. Why this scripture? When there's a *why* to the reason, you will own the scripture!

Chapter *12*

"Time":
A Valuable Resource

> ⟶ ⟵

During my restoration, I picked up valuable resources that were very helpful in my journey. The most valuable is *time*. I learned that God is a restorer of time and what you give to Him, graciously He gives back threefold. The more I spent in His presence, the more I seemed to get accomplished. I realized that just as He rebukes the devourer in our finances, He also rebukes the devourer of our time. I began to monitor the time I spent in prayer. I would begin my prayer at 7:00 am and before I knew it, the time was 8:00 or 8:30 am. I would listen to songs in worship and speak in my prayer language in route to work, that would be approximately thirty minutes. Then at night, before bed, I would get lost in my payer time. I would journal while in meditative prayer. I began to learn that my days were more relaxed. I was able to get more out of my days. So, I calculated my time in prayer and realized that unconsciously, I was spending 2 ½ -3 hours of my day in prayer and I was getting more done with less effort. Now, I share this to help you understand the power we possess as Believers. As Believers, God restores us.

To make better use of my prayer time, I strategize. I turn off all noise and enter a quiet area. My preferred prayer place is my dining room. I am usually hidden from the distractions of everyone getting dressed for school and work, and I am able to finish and go quickly into the kitchen to get breakfast finished. My journal and Bible is the only thing I take to prayer. I open up with a scripture verse. Some mornings, I will read a daily prayer. Then, I begin to pray. I start by thanking my Father for everything He's already done and for what He is about to do. During scripture reading, I am led to pray for someone or something. I typically listen and allow the Holy Spirit to direct and guide me. When I make my prayer time led by the Holy Spirit, I stay about my Father's business.

AND WE RECOVERED ALL...

Reconstruction

―――――――⊙⟨⟩⟨⟩⊙―――――――

"Failure is a great teacher, and I think when you make mistakes and you recover from them and you treat them as valuable learning experiences, then you've got something to share." ~Steve Harvey

Chapter *13*

Taking Back My Family

"...And He answered him, "Pursue, for you shall surely overtake them, and without fail recover all." 1Samuel 30:8(KJV)

> ✦

When I read about the life of David, it brings chills to my spine. When I read the second passage of 1Samuel 30:8, I did not include the full scripture. David asked first and God told him without fail, he will **recover all**. Praise the Lord! I encourage you to find a scripture and hold on to it for dear life. When the changes began to take place in my home, I wanted to run. I was tired and worn out and did not have the stomach to fight. Some people told me it was because of Darrick being too strict and others told me it was because I was too lenient or simply put, we were not on the same accord. I felt it was my fault and I felt like a complete failure. I was dealing with bad grades, bad attitudes, and rebellious spirits. When I walked in the bookstores, it seemed as if every book I grabbed gave me no quick answers.

So, the bickering between Darrick and I started again. He would compare me to his mother and I would go into attack mode.

None of this helped the situation; it was as if the kids were looking at us and laughing mocking, "I told you so." For the first time, I felt I was fighting for something and God was telling me to let it go. Was I holding on for fear of being alone or was I truly holding on because God told me to? Was I gaining a husband and losing my children? What was going on? The Holy Spirit immediately gave me a scripture, be wise of the attacks of the enemy for he comes to kill. John 10:10 (KJV) says," The thief cometh not, but for to steal, and to kill, and to destroy: I am come that they might have life, and that they might have it more abundantly."

＞ ＜

Light Bulb Moment!

Satan will use whomever to take you off course.

＞ ＜

I had to talk to my children. I had to fight, I had to put on the whole armor of God and prepare myself for battle, because I was not going to lose my children or my spouse. God told me to get a scripture and hold on to it. I did just that. I read 1 Samuel 30, the story of David when he smites the Amalekites. In verse four, David and his men wept, in verse six, David encouraged himself in the Lord his God. And in verse eight, he asked the Lord should he pursue and the Lord answered: "Pursue; for thou shalt surely overtake them, and without fail recover all." In verse nineteen, David recovered all. I held on to this passage, these verses. I replaced David with my name and recited: "And Nycholle recovered all!" I never lost sight of the goal to recover all and neither will you. I just had to properly prepare for battle. Yes, we both had to show our children the love of the Lord and that He lives in us.

I have to ask you to jot down a scripture that will help you, re-place any name or pronoun with your name, as I did above. Pray for your children, your spouse, and anyone else that you have given power to whether it's a parent or in-law. Pray for strength. I had more talks with God during this time in my life than I ever have. I prayed in the car, in the bathroom, and in the bedroom. Some-times, I would just think about things and before I knew it, I was talking to the Lord about it. Not once did He not answer me. It may not have been in my time, but they were all answered in His timing. I highlighted passages in my Bible for every situation I was going through. There were songs I would sing to make a joyful noise unto the Lord, even when I didn't feel like it. I began to like my own melody's more than what was on the radio. Things began to get a little easier.

I held on to Romans 12 Christian conduct as my guide, particu-larly verse 12: "Rejoice and exult in hope; be steadfast and patient in suffering and tribulation: be constant in prayer." I was consistent in my prayer life and I could see things; God revealed things that were going to come to pass that I had to let go and allow to happen. I had to watch my children experience things that, as a mother, you don't want to see occur, but God told me He knew what He needed to allow to happen to me, in order for me to get to Him, and the same went for my children. He knew what He needed to allow in their lives for them to come to Him. I had to intercede on behalf of my children and I had to, in so many ways, let go. Letting go was my way of surrendering them to my Heaven-ly Father, knowing that I am their earthly mother. But He is their Heavenly Father and I could not want more for them in my finite mind, than He could. So, I had to trust the process. I watched His mighty hand work in the lives of my children. Malachi 4:6 says, "And He shall turn the heart of the fathers to the children, and the heart of the children to their fathers, lest I come and smite the earth with a curse." My prayers were answered and relationships restored. Hallelujah, was it easy? No, it was hard, but the lessons were learned that I could never have taught. The hand of God on their lives will bless them for generations.

Chapter 14

Testimony/Forgiveness

"Moreover whom He predestined, these He also called;
whom He called, these He also justified; and whom He justified,
these He also glorified." Romans 8:30

Our lives have been forever restored because of our belief in God and His ability to heal our marriage. Our healing came at a time that pastors we looked up to in the media were divorcing. It's devastating for couples who are looking for strength in strong pastors, see pastors divorce. It was also a learning lesson for me because you can't put so much pressure on pastors; they are human beings just like you and I. I value the covenant and this commitment and it does not mean that they don't; it means that God put something in me to share with the world, to help others, and that is what I am called to do. I walk through church sometimes and I can see the couples, like us, how we use to be. I can see there is no love or it's just been buried by neglect and life. It does not have to be that way.

We worked overtime to put our marriage back together again and my only regret is that it took us so long. I placed more value on education and my appearance, than on my marriage. I pray God will give us back the years we lost, so that we can show our children's children what love is. That it is more than saying I love you. It means understanding that we are one flesh, that as one flesh if you lose one of your five toes, it will impact the way you walk, or stand. Like the one toe, without Darrick, I am incomplete. I recognized that the love I have for him transcended over the years. It took on many forms, but the one thing that remains is my unconditional love. I can go to him with my daily struggles and he will encourage me. I can trust my tears with him and him with me and know that what hurts him hurts me. It is respecting one another in the presence or absence of one another. Sometimes, this love took on a strong form of dislike or contention, but we were able to survive it. When people tell me they are thinking of divorce, I tell them our story. I ask them first, "Do you love the Lord? The answer is usually, "Yes." Then, I share my scriptural passage.

> ❖

Light Bulb Moment!

Find a scripture, hold on tight, and keep it close.

> ❖

I share with them that if you love the Lord and believe every promise written in the Bible to be true, find a scripture and hold on tight. If you don't have one, here is mine. My passage, the very reason for this book, the story of the *Dry Bones*, I will print in its entirety because when people ask me how we made it, this is my answer, "I read Ezekiel 37." And when I say I read Ezekiel, I do; I pull up my Bible app on my phone and I read it with compassion, with heart, and with promise, because it is the Word of God. I let the scripture saturate the very heart, eyes, and ears because it is my testimony, it is my story. Ezekiel 37:1-14 (AMP) says, "THE HAND of the Lord was upon me, and He brought me out in the Spirit of the Lord and set me down in the midst of the valley; and it was full of bones. And He caused me to pass round about among them, and behold, there were very many [human bones] in the open valley or plain, and behold, they were very dry. And He said to me, Son of man, can these bones live? And I answered, O Lord God, You know! Again He said to me, Prophesy to these bones and say to them, O you dry bones, hear the word of the Lord. Thus says the Lord God to these bones: Behold, I will cause breath and spirit to enter you, and you shall live; And I will lay sinews upon you and bring up flesh upon you and cover you with skin, and I will put breath and spirit in you, and you [dry bones] shall live; and you shall know, understand, and realize that I am the Lord [the Sovereign Ruler, Who calls forth loyalty and obedient service]. So I prophesied as I was commanded; and as I prophesied, there was a [thundering] noise and behold, a shaking and trembling and a rattling, and the bones came together, bone to its bone. And I looked and behold, there were sinews upon [the bones] and flesh came upon them and skin covered them over, but there was no breath or spirit in them. Then said He to me, Prophesy to the breath and spirit, son of man, and say to the breath and spirit, Thus says the Lord God: Come from the four winds, O breath and spirit, and breathe upon these slain that they may live. So I prophesied as He commanded me, and the breath and spirit came into [the bones], and they lived and stood up upon their feet, an exceedingly great host. Then He said to me, Son of man, these bones are the whole house of Israel. Behold, they say, Our bones are dried up and our hope is lost; we are completely cut off. Therefore prophesy and say to them, Thus says the Lord God: Behold, I will open your graves and cause you to come up out of your graves, O My people; and I will bring you [back home] to the land of Israel. And you shall know that I am the Lord [your Sovereign Ruler], when I have opened your graves and caused you to come up out of your graves, O My people. And I shall put My Spirit in you and you shall live, and I shall place you in your own land. Then you shall know, understand, and realize that I the Lord have spoken it and performed it, says the Lord."

If an army of dry bones, in the desert, can rise and live based on the power of spoken word and become an army, I know prophesying in my marriage could bring life back into it! Prophesy Nycholle, prophesy! Can these bones live? O ye dry bones, hear the word of the Lord. The first time the Lord gave me this passage; my initial reaction was I had not spoken life into my dead marriage. I toyed with entitling this book Dry Bones because that is what I tell everyone, *Dry Bones.* As I came to the final days of writing, I realized the book, my testimony, is based on *Reconstruction* to the *Restoration* of an army of Dry Bones by speaking the Living Word of God, as in the passage of the Valley of Dry Bones. I say unto you if you believe in your heart of hearts that the Lord can reconstruct and restore your marriage and your family for His glory, He can. He will do what His Word says for He is not a man that will lie. Ephesians 3:20-21 (KJV) says, "Now unto him that is able to do exceeding abundantly above all that we ask or think, according to the power that worketh in us, Unto him be glory in the church by Christ Jesus throughout all ages, world without end. Amen."

Don't just pray for recovery, pray for reconstruction because you don't want a repaired version of yourselves; you want a reconstructed version, reconstructed the way God intended you to be. Living, standing, and trusting on His Word was enough for me to believe, because I just wanted my marriage to be whole and healthy. But His Word says that He is able to do all that I ask or can think. Wow! Can you think it? God can increase me more than I can even fathom in my finite mind. My mind is limited to what my eyes have been exposed to. My God wants to bless me beyond my own comprehension. Glory! So, I don't limit God's healing; I do the work and some days, I am amazed at the things He blesses my household with. We are not perfect people, Darrick and I mess up, but the difference is we don't sit and remain content with the state of happiness we're in today. No, I expect greater today than I had yesterday. I expect more because the Word says that He is able to do exceedingly... above all I can think. The expectation increases daily. Hallelujah! Do I have a definition of greater? No, because even though I understand the Word, I don't expect, I know, it will be greater!

Isaiah 43:19 (KJV) says, "Behold, I will do a new thing; now it shall spring forth; shall ye not know it? I will even make a way in the wilderness, and rivers in the desert." Now, I don't know about you, but I lived in the country, so I know what a wilderness looks like. You can walk in the wilderness and literally get lost, but my God says He will make a way in the wilderness, and rivers in the desert. Look over the promises of God in the Old and New Testament and simply input your name and your spouse's name to the verse and prophesy!

Light Bulb Moment!

God works on logistics and strategy to bless the masses.

As of 2013, the world population was estimated at 7.13 billion people based on WorldoMeter.com[ix]. I am unaware of the accuracy of the numbers; however, the information is not being used for statistical data. I am merely adding that Darrick and I are two individuals in a world of 7.13 billion. God's never looking to simply bless two people; He works on multiplication and division. He guided us on the journey of restoration and healing not to simply bless my home; He wants us to give hope to others. God's blessings are to bless a generation, to bring new Believers to the Body of Christ. If we think of God in terms of the number of people in the world, He is the Almighty and Omnipresent God who sees all. He works on logistics and strategies to effectively bless the masses. Remember, He's not adding and subtracting; His blessing multiplies exponentially.

Let's think of God in a matter of business. Most of us work or understand the concept of business operations. Typically in business, there is the Board of Directors, CEO, CFO, Manager, Supervisors, and Employees. Well in business, a company survives based on the amount of money they are able to show the Board of Directors. They typically want to show growth. The Board of Directors is usually made up of investors and they have a genuine interest in the business success, and normally that interest is money. When a company ceases to make or generate a positive flow of money, the company will become bankrupt; stocks and the value in the company is low and folds, or goes under. To avoid loss of revenue, the Board of Directors will vote to resign a CEO and in some cases, the CFO, to develop a fresh strategy to keep the company in the red, or growing. Sometimes, when a company hires a well-known successful CEO, just announcing the news will increase the value or stock in that company. There are times when the CEO will restructure the strategy, or logistics of the company, to become more efficient, allowing the product to reach the largest amount of people proficiently. Well, I liken God's position in my home to that of a business. I believe God's position in my home is like that of the Board of Directors, and His board consists of God the Father, God the Son, and the Holy Spirit, aka The Trinity. Well, our restoration of our marriage was much like that of restructuring a failing company. We were going under fast.

Light Bulb Moment!

The Board of Directors was not getting a return on their investments.

Our lifestyle was winning more souls for the darkness and no one was looking at our lives and wanting to know our God. The Board decided we had to redefine our mission statement. The first step was to understand we all had clearly defined roles established before Darrick and I were born. In restructuring, Darrick was repositioned to CEO; he was tasked with ensuring our home gets a return for the Board of Directors. Now, the Board wants to ensure our marriage stays intact and that the Board of Directors gets the glory. The Board meets with us daily to ensure we are aligned with the mission statement and yield to the prompting of the Holy Spirit. In business, we understand we must yield to the CEO; we typically dress in business formal when the CEO is visiting. We automatically respect the authority and position he/she holds with that title. Well, as my husband, Darrick has earned the title of CEO in our home. I am his helpmate, and as his helpmate, I was made for him. I was designed to help him. This does not mean that I don't have my own identity, ideas, or desires; it simply means that together we are a union, and I am here to help and not hurt him.

I am the CFO. As the CFO, I can't have my own agenda or go against the mission of our home, so I yield to the prompting of the Holy Spirit and He guides me daily. I am submitted to my husband, but I am not powerless. One of his day to day goals is to ensure our home is prospering holistically. He makes decisions based upon the home flowing and prospering. Once you grasp this, you will ensure an investment to your Board of Directors. When you focus first on God, you realize your first ministry is your home, then everything else flows the way it should.

Your minor children are employees, hourly or salary. I would like to say that minor children are the hourly employees and the teenagers are salaried employees. The CEO establishes rules and regulations that allow the home to run smoothly; in businesses, they are called Standard Operating Procedures (SOP's). In our home, I call them contracts. When you run your home like you're a business, you will learn that there are fewer opportunities to fail. Your covering is in place when your home is in order and you are in position for a blessing. I learned early to use a contract to run my home efficiently. When you run your home like a business, it prospers.

> ← →

Light Bulb Moment!

Stay Encouraged.

> ← →

Focus on scriptures that give you a reason to stay. Avoid making compare and contrast lists of reasons to stay versus reasons to leave, because if you want out of a marriage, you will find reasons to leave. If you don't have reasons to stay based upon what he or she has done, then go to the Bible and find reasons to stay. List scriptures to recite when doubt comes in and recite them. There are so many Bibles that are written for specific issues. There's a Bible by T.D. Jakes, it's the NKJV *Woman Thou Art Loosed Edition.* [x]This Bible lists scriptures for the specific issue you are facing. The hard work has been completed for you; all you need to do is copy the scripture on an index card and carry it with you until it gets in your spirit.

Every Man's Bible, A Bible for Every Battle Every Man Faces by Stephen Arterburn and Dean Merrill[xi] is also a helpful resource. There are many electronic/digital supports that helped me, like *The Holy Bible app*; *You Version* has plans to read that give you daily scripture to encourage you. *BibleGateway.com* is an excellent online resource. If you want help, the information is out there. You just have to open your eyes and purpose to find it. 2 Timothy 2:15 (KJV) says, "Study to shew thyself approved unto God, a workman that needeth not to be ashamed, rightly dividing the word of truth."

I remember having a conversation with the Lord and saying, "You told me to prophesy, I did! You told me you would give me the desires of my heart, I am expecting the desires of my heart!

You said the prayers of the righteous availeth much; my prayers will not return to me void!" I recited back the Word of God to Him. Who am I to tell God what He said He would do? I said a few things and had to repent a few times, but I got angry at my situation, angry at my circumstances, and I would call on the name of Jesus and He answered. You have to call on the name of Jesus not your friends, family, or even your parents. You have to study His Word and you have to thank Him daily for what He is doing in your life, no matter how small.

I share with you that divorce is on the rise; it is our duty and responsibility to make our marriage work. Life is not 50/50; if you give 50% and your spouse gives 50%, you will not have a marriage. When marriage is based on 100/100 you get one, One Flesh. You have a whole being made up of two whole beings of like mind and spirit. We are living in a world where self-help and diet and weight loss books are number one best sellers. We have forgotten about foundational promises of the Bible. We have forgotten that we serve a mighty God and I will repeat, Ephesians 3:20-21 (Message): "God can do anything, you know—far more than you could ever imagine or guess or request in your wildest dreams! He does it not by pushing us around but by working within us, his Spirit deeply and gently within us."

The Message Bible breaks the passage down, writing we could not even imagine in our wildest dreams. Hallelujah! We have the tools at our disposal to make our marriage work and it begins with our mouth. We simply must access the power that works in us to speak life, and not death. To *prophesy*, according to Merriam-Webster, is defined as to utter by or as if by divine inspiration. So you have the scripture, which is divine inspiration, and all you need to do is utter, or speak. You must choose to speak life in your marriage, in your home, and in your children, as if your life depends upon it. I choose affirmations that are biblically sound that I recite daily. I speak life in everything I do.

God's Word will grow you more than any book, prescription, or counselor could ever do. God's Living Word is called *living* for a reason. I have lain on my face crying out to the Lord for a Word and got up from prayer, opened the Living Word, and a scripture was right on the page that clearly spoke to the issue I was having. The more you read the Word, pray, and prophesy in your life, you will find the inner happiness you seek. No college degree could ever give me the confidence to write this book, prophesy to save my marriage, or take my children from a dysfunctional home to a home of love. My confidence is a result of living the Word of God, seeking a scripture to apply to my life, and walking in my divine given right to have a life of abundance and expect more today, than I had yesterday. To God be the glory!

I have been told that I am a woman of influence. Well, I don't know that to be true, but I share the Word of God. I am confident that in any situation or circumstance we face, there is a Word that will heal you. To walk in this authority or healing, we must first be able to forgive. You cannot expect to receive the blessings of the Lord without forgiveness. Forgiveness is needed; otherwise, you will always be held back from receiving the promises of the Lord.

Forgiveness is the key to allowing any marriage to work. Some people say I may forgive, but I don't forget. I hate that response; it is in direct conflict with the Word of God. Again, I am only a Bible toting Momma, but I don't believe we should not forget. The Bible shows a cause-effect relationship towards forgiveness in Matthew

6:14-15 (KJV), "For if ye forgive men their trespasses, your heavenly Father will also forgive you: But if ye forgive not men their trespasses, neither will your Father forgive your trespasses." Now, I will include the Amplified version: Matthew 6:14-15 (AMP), "For if you forgive people their trespasses [their reckless and willful sins, leaving them, letting them go, and giving up resentment], your heavenly Father will also forgive you. But if you do not forgive others their trespasses [their reckless and willful sins, leaving them, letting them go, and giving up resentment], neither will your Father forgive you your trespasses". In the Lord's Prayer or Matthew 6:12 (KJV), "And forgive us our debts, as we forgive our debtors." Again, forgiveness is mentioned in Luke 6:37-38 (KJV): "Judge not, and ye shall not be judged: condemn not, and ye shall not be condemned: forgive, and ye shall be forgiven: Give and it shall be given unto you; good measure, pressed down, and shaken together, and running over, shall men give into your bosom. For with the same measure that ye mete withal it shall be measured to you again."

Merriam-Webster defines *forgive* as to give up resentment of or claim to requital for an insult. They go on to define *forget* as to lose the remembrance of: be unable to think or recall. Clearly, forgiveness is contingent on forgetting. If you're unable to think or recall, it means you forgot the information. When you are able to recall something, you have not released it and it will visit you again. It will take hold of your mind and make you captive to the scent, the touch, the taste, the visual, and impact how you feel. Let it go! Pray to Abba Father to allow you to forget the way you know He forgets your sin. Micah 7:19 (KJV) says, "He will turn again, he will have compassion upon us; he will subdue our iniquities; and thou wilt cast all their sins into the depths of the sea." When we think of this scripture *God will cast our sins into the depths of the sea*, it implies they are forgotten. Are we God? No, but we are like God, because His Spirit lives within us.

In Psalms 103:12 (KJV), we are told: "As far as the east is from the west, so far hath he removed our transgressions from us." Scripture tells us that God will forget our sins. If we don't believe this, then we can never go boldly before the throne, naked and broken, and believe God is just to forgive us and believe that we are entitled to anything written in the Book of Life. You can't truly forgive, unless you forget. When you don't try to consciously forget mistreatments of others and even of your own doing, you will forever give the enemy power over you. Our senses are very strong; we have five senses and others have six; some call it a *sixth sense*. These senses can be used to wreak havoc in your life as constant reminders of negative instances in your life. I am not saying you walk around and if you've been robbed, you shouldn't be conscious of your senses and sixth sense, or gut feeling, that something is wrong. Obviously, you want to be conscious of your surroundings. I am speaking to the smell of cologne that brings back a negative remembrance to the point that when you smell it, everyone recalls what you are feeling and you relive that event in your mind and then it festers in your attitude towards the person. We must free our minds from the enemy to walk in total forgiveness that we want God to forgive us. You have to operate in the now! In order to live in the now, right now in regards to time and space, you can't be in the past. The past holds memories. Energy is wasted on rehearsing old emotions.

When I think of the things I have done in my life and all the times I have asked God to forgive me, I don't want Him to say, "Oh no daughter, you are not forgiven because you just did this last week or last year." Many months I held on to the things I asked God to forgive me for and since I did not forgive myself, I held myself in bondage to the sin. I could not go boldly before the Lord to ask for anything, because my inability to truly forgive myself left me broken without hope. I want to be able to walk boldly before my Lord and Savior knowing when I fall, He is looking at me now and not last year. I don't pray in fear. I pray knowing that I am a righteous woman of the Most High God and I know He has forgiven me in the matter I have forgiven. In Ephesians 6:10-18 we discussed earlier the Whole Armor of God, but I would like to point out something that is important. Our senses are touch, smell, hear, taste, visual, and a "sixth sense" I call *intuition* or *spiritual awareness*.

Now I feel like an Elementary teacher, but here's a visual, the Armor of God is likened to the armor of a Roman Soldier; the Belt of Truth (loins girt about with truth), the Breastplate of Righteousness (guards our heart), Gospel of Peace (feet shod), Shield of Faith (blocks visual attacks), the Helmet of Salvation (guards our thoughts) , the Sword of the Spirit (the Word of God), and finally the Power of Praying (mouth/speech). It takes all the elements of the Armor of God to attack the senses. But, we can never protect ourselves by putting on superficial armor; we must be in right standing to be able to put on the whole armor and that comes with forgiveness. Understand, people will not understand why you are forgiving, why you are changing; no one likes change, even positive change, so be prepared to give a logical response and the Word has prepared us for this. 1Peter 3:15 AMP says, "But in your hearts set Christ apart as holy [and acknowledge Him] as Lord. Always be ready to give a logical defense to anyone who asks you to account for the hope that is in you, but do it courteously and respectfully."

For we know that God has equipped us with His Word and His grace and it's all we need! This battle is not ours to fight, we stand on Hebrew 4:12 AMP, which tells us "For the Word that God speaks is alive and full of power [making it active, operative, energizing, and effective]; it is sharper than any two-edged sword, penetrating to the dividing line of the breath of life (soul) and [the immortal] spirit, and of joints and marrow [of the deepest parts of our nature], exposing and sifting and analyzing and judging the very thoughts and purposes of the heart." I chose the Amplified Version here because it describes the power of the Word of God. Give God some praise, Hallelujah!

Chapter *15*

The Ultimate Blessing

"But it is written: Eyes have not seen, nor ear heard, Nor have entered into the heart of man The things which God has prepared for those who love Him." 1 Corinthians 2:9

❖ ❖

When you get to the point where you trust the Lord and your family grows together, it is wonderful. We have a connection now, but true blessing is not just within the constraints of your own home; they go outside the walls of your home and family. My eldest daughter was in a relationship with a young man that I did not believe was worthy of her time. I felt I should not discourage the relationship because it would only strengthen the relationship. I remember the Lord telling me to pray for this young man; I actually questioned the Lord why I should pray for this man who has caused me such grief and agony? Of course, I did not get a response, so I got out of my bed and as obedient as I was, got on my knees and said, "Lord, bless this young man, Amen." I went back to bed knowing I had not done what the Lord wanted and yet I did as He asked. A little play on words here, but I want to be real. We have to yield ourselves to the prompting of the Lord and when He told me to pray, I knew what He wanted; He wanted intercessory prayer. He wanted me to cry out for this young man, and I couldn't even fake it.

Sometimes, the very uncomfortable thing God wants us to do will cause us to grow. The next day, the Lord led me to the story of Saul as he was rejected as King, the story found in 1 Samuel 15:22: "Has the Lord as great delight in burnt offerings and sacrifices, As in obeying the voice of the Lord? Behold to obey is better than sacrifice." How dare I challenge the burden God placed on my heart and question what He called me to do? Who was I to ask that He restore my daughter and yet I could not pray for His son. I had to ask God to forgive me. I didn't drop down on my knees to pray for the young man, but I had hoped God would allow me to be obedient. Exactly 2:00 a.m. the next morning, I was awakened to pray for the young man. I got on my knees and prayed a heartfelt prayer for this young man; I cried out and interceded for him in a way that even I was surprised. I held contempt for this young man and I had no love for him, but the Lord gave me a burden and softened my heart.

Previously, I thought of things I would say to him if I saw him that were not very fruitful. However, all of those thoughts escaped me, because I was praying for this man asking the Lord to give him what He needs. Within two days, my daughter and this young man broke up. My daughter later told me that she did not understand why he had such control over her. I had to pray to break that bondage. I find myself, even now, being led to pray for him. In that moment, I learned God had prepared me for this very situation. He prepared me by showing me how to trust in Him. I was able to learn to lay my cares upon Him and trust that He would restore without a shadow of doubt. I have been in the store and blessed people by giving the cashier a gift card to give the family, or doing stuff that caused me to say, "But are you sure?" I try to operate in the Spirit. One of the many arguments my husband and I would have was on giving to the homeless. He would say they are con-artists and I would argue that it's not my place to say they are or not, but when you operate in the Spirit, you know when the need is financial versus prayer or just a hug. Even my husband now blesses these brothers and sisters he believed were all "cons". We have a healthy balance of who we are and we yield to the will of God, no matter what.

I used to ask why we had to experience lack, division, and contention in our marriage. Why did we have to lose each other to find one another again? As I write this book, I see the full picture. We had to go through everything we experienced to see the fullness of our Lord and the power of prayer. I think of Moses and leading the children of Israel out of Egypt. Pharaoh's heart was hardened so the people could see the miracles of the Lord. My journey was similar; it was to show me, our family, that God is a restorer. I would not have known I could pray negative people out of the lives of my children or speak life in the lives of those who think divorce is inevitable. When couples tell me they are thinking of divorce, I minister to them. I want my marriage to be a beacon to others. I want God to use us to show others that in this 21st century, true love still exists. If I had not learned to put the Lord first to establish a relationship to see beyond the surface and pull up the root of bitterness, both Darrick and I would have been lost forever. When my children go through the growing pains of adulthood, I can lead them to a scripture. I can intercede on their behalf through prayer and I can live a life that is pleasing in the eyes of God, so He will use me. I am so thankful for going through this situation, because it helped me to see the full glory of the Lord. I was able to see God's glory extend beyond my walls and beyond whom I thought God had given me authority over. That's when I realized God called me to intercessory prayer, and my prayer is to restore homes and families. I am so thankful that one day I was lost and in a time of confusion; God showed me that He is not a God of confusion and showed me the Valley of Dry Bones. I am thankful that I had not understood the fullness of the passage, until I was a willing vessel, ready to receive what *thus saith the Lord*.

I often feel like we're in the minority. I talk to couples and I see T.V. "Did you consult T.V. personalities when you wanted to get married." Why do we feel the need to minimize the power of God in the healing and restoration of our marriages? Our task in sharing our story is to show that restoration is possible. Is it hard work? Absolutely, but nothing worth having is ever easy. We reached out to the Lord, and our healing was very much like David's. We wept, we asked God, and we recovered all!

Chapter *16*

Letter of Apology

"Confess your faults one to another, and pray one for another, that ye may be healed. The effectual fervent prayer of a righteous man availeth much." James 5:16 (KJV)

—— ✦ ✦ ——

As a wife, mother, sister, and daughter, I was not leading a life by example. I think of the many lives I touched negatively. The daughters, my daughters, and sons who watched me transform in front of their eyes. I had no regard for the women I came in contact with. I introduced them to deception. As a woman of God, I am instructed to live a life to teach others. Titus 2:3-5 says, "The aged women likewise, that they be in behavior as becometh holiness, not false accusers, not given to much wine, teachers of good things; That they may teach the young women to be sober, to love their husbands, to love their children, To be discreet, chaste, keepers at home, good, obedient to their own husbands, that the word of God be not blasphemed." We devalue the holy Word of God when we don't honor our sisters and brothers by demonstrating fruitful behavior. I am to demonstrate the wife my sons will someday marry or the wives my daughters will someday become. There are many examples of ungodly behavior demonstrated in the world; however, as a woman of God, I am to let my light shine. Writing this book, I have been married for nineteen years and I have enjoyed young men approaching me saying they want a wife that will display the characteristics I possess. When I think about that, it confirms people are watching us. We may be the only example of a mother or wife people will see. When you realize your true place or position in life, you see the many lives you touch along the way. I apologize to all the men and women I deceived in my past, but I thank God for renewing me and calling me into the woman I am today. I am thankful that God does not operate in subtraction and addition, but multiplies our value.

B O O K   M A R K   A F F I R M A T I O N S

"And I will restore to you the years that the locust hath eaten, the cankerworm, and the caterpillar, and the palmerworm, my great army which I sent among you." Joel 2:25

Mrs.	Mr.
I am a woman of God.	I am a man of God.
I will restore my covenant.	I will restore my covenant.
My marriage will please God.	My marriage will please God.
We have a testimony to share with others.	We have a testimony to share with others.
I love my husband.	I love my wife.
God is a restorer.	God is a restorer.
My children will experience our restoration.	My children will experience our restoration.
We're creating a legacy.	We're creating a legacy.
I will give 100%.	I will give 100%.
It worked for Nycholle.	It worked for Darrick.

Joel 2:25-26	Joel 2:25-26
1John 5:4	1John 5:4
Isaiah 61:7	Isaiah 61:7
Job 42:10	Job 42:10
1 Corinthians 7:10-11	1Peter 3:7
Titus 2:1-15	Titus 2:1-15
1 John 4:18	Matthew 19:8
Philippians 4:8	Philippians 4:8
1 Corinthians 13:7	1 Corinthians 13:7

Library

Change your library to include books that will lift your spirit. Trade in the romance novels for biblical resources. Keep your mind focused on things that will lift your spirit. Philippians 4:8 (KJV) says, "Finally, brethren, whatsoever things are true, whatsoever things are honest, whatsoever things are just, whatsoever things are pure, whatsoever things are lovely, whatsoever things are of good report; if there be any virtue, and if there be any praise, think on these things." I found novels that encouraged me. Music also changed to upbeat Jazz, Instrumental, Gospel, and Christian. I guarded what entered my ear gate. Most people don't realize the power of stories/novels we read, music we listen to, and movies we watch, can change our thinking. If the music you listen to is lustful, you will find that you're attracting people to you, because that spirit is on you. Novels will make you believe you lack passion and romance in your marriage. Don't let your senses take you on a roller coaster before your restoration is complete.

Affirmations & Declarations

I am a firm believer in affirmations. Every year, I create a family affirmation and revisit it to make necessary changes throughout the year. I have one for my family, one for myself, and one for my career goals. I encourage you to write a family declaration. I will give you my first affirmation. I wrote this during the *Reconstruction* phase of my life.

"I declare the year of 2007 to be a year of blessings and prosperity. I will walk by faith and not by sight. I declare no weapon shall form against me for I am more than a conqueror through Jesus Christ. I have been brought with a price. Scripture says for no man who believes in Him [adhers to, relies on, trust in Christ] will [ever] be put to shame or be disappointed. Roman 10:11(AMP) For I know that I am the temple of God and the Spirit of God dwells in me, 1 Corinthians 3:16 (AMP). All of my household shall be of the same mind (one mind) having compassion for one another, love as brethren, be pitiful, and be courteous. 1 Peter 3:8 (AMP) I will close the doors of division. Create an atmosphere of unity. Build strong marriage, be the light to others. Increased blessings for our children. Teach them to love themselves and each other. I declare that God is head of my life and I commit my family to His will in Jesus name. Amen! 1/1/2007 I will recover all!!

My declaration is on the screen of my laptop, cell phone, and at the front of my daily planner. I read and recite it every day. Every year around November, I assess the New Year and begin to look over all God has done for my family. I see release every year. So over the years, I have grown more specific and direct with my declaration. My declaration for 2013.

Scripture tells me, For no man who believes in Him [adheres to, relies on, trust in Christ] will [ever] be put to shame or be disappointed Roman 10:11 Believing the Word of God, I declare:

2013 will be the year of Abundance in wealth, health, prosperity, and wisdom. I have and experience abundance in:

• <u>Wealth</u>: For my family and I are lenders and not borrowers; we owe no man nothing; for we are good stewards of God's money.

• <u>Health</u>: My family and I are healthy, our bodies have a balance of healthy red and white blood cells doing what they are designed to do: heal and repair! Our weight is normal and bone density is correct, skin is free of imperfections, our bodies are rejuvenated to allow only the input of healthy substances. Our intestines are working to expel what it does not need and retain what it does. Blood sugar levels are normal and kidneys are functioning perfectly. Lungs expand and retract as they should. Nerves are synapse the way they should and signals are being sent and received, healthy and normal. We are blessed with sound mind. Speech is flawless articulating words that effect positive change and produce fruit to the listener! Mind, body, and spirit is healthy!

• <u>Prosperity</u>: Successful and prosperous in home, work, church and community.

• <u>Wisdom</u>: I am virtuous woman! My girls, Brittany and Amber, are virtuous women of God. We handle finances, homemaking, and community responsibilities with grace and humility. We manage our time and talent wisely, using it to glorify God! We are respected among our peers as women who influence greatness and have a genuine love for the Lord. We do not speak negative against our brothers and sisters, but ask God how He can better use us to glorify His Kingdom. Darrick is a strong man of God. He is leading his sons, Colby and Devin, into manhood and men to the Lord by his actions and his own personal relationship with the Lord. Colby and Devin are leaders, men standing in the GAP recognizing a need within the community and fulfilling it. They are Leaders and not followers. We are all fearfully and wonderfully made; we are a direct reflection of God's own heart! We have a direct connection to God via the Spirit that lives within us. Thank you Father for wisdom and understanding in knowing this.

For we believe Isaiah 54:17: "No weapon that is formed against us shall prosper, and every tongue that shall rise against us in judgment I shall show to be in the wrong. This is the heritage of the servants of the Lord, and their righteousness is from me, says the Lord."

For I know that I am temple of God and the Spirit of God dwells within me as written in 1 Corinthians 3:16. All of my household shall be of the same mind (one mind) having compassion for one another, love as brethren, be pitiful, and be courteous. 1 Peter 3:8. We will close the doors of division and open the doors of unity and one mind! Create an atmosphere of unity. Build a strong marriage and be a light/ beacon to others. Increase blessings for our children and their children. Teach them to love themselves and each other. I declare that God is the head of my life and I commit myself, my family and my circle/realm of influence to His will! I declare that by my own might none of this is possible, but possibility exists because we serve a mighty God and through Him, working in us, all things are possible for those who believe and are with God, because it's written! Matthew 19:26: "But Jesus looked at them and said, with men this is impossible, but all things are possible with God." Again in Mark 9:23: "And Jesus said, [You say to Me], If you can do anything? [Why,] all things can be (are possible) to him who believes." Again in Mark 10:27: "Jesus glanced around at them and said, With men [it is] impossible, but not with God; for all things are possible with God." There are no mistakes or typos… all things are possible with God. AMEN! I believe it! I receive it!"

Glory to the Lord! Thank you for giving us eyes to see and ears to hear and a heart to receive what the Lord says. Now, as I look at my year of 2013 with the inception of new ideas and "God Assignments," I will be clear and precise with my Declaration for 2014, and so on. Now if you don't have one, then I suggest you change the wording of mine until you create your own. My Pastor had us to write our declaration and read it three times a day. Well, he did not see mine. So, I copied my declaration in my phone as an appointment that alarms at 9:00 am, 12 noon, and 6:00 pm. Now when I worked, I had calculated down to the minute how long it took me to read. It would take me three minutes to read it with heart and compassion, and not just read or recite from memory. I need to get it in my spirit. So I, too, encourage you to write your declaration and affirmation and put it in your calendar to recite it daily, post it on your bathroom mirror, and recite it while getting dressed. However you choose to read your declaration, make sure you do so with compassion and expectancy. I did not get to this point by reciting; I got to this point by holding onto every word with expectancy!

Chapter *17*

Document Your Progress

"Therefore do not be unwise, but understand what the will of the Lord is." Ephesians 5:17

＞＜

Keeping track of your progress is important. Your journal is a compass to guide you, a map to track where you've been. Think of it as a frame of reference to measure your journey of restoration.

You will need a five subject, college-ruled notebook, and write on the page something similar to what I have written below. I have included one of the passages from my journal entry as a guide.

Date: 1/12/2007

What I Read: Exodus 4:21

What I Marked: God is all knowing, all powerful. Why did He harden the heart of Pharaoh and not allow/make Pharaoh to release the children of Israel? Why am I going through this? Is God hardening Darrick's heart towards me?

What it Means: God had done many miracles when He led Israel out of Egypt; however, God is an awesome, wondrous, powerful God. He tells Moses He will harden Pharaoh's heart so he will not let Israel go. With my limited understanding of theology, I realized that: 1. God needed Israel to see the miracles performed, 2. God needed Israel to know that the leader, or the anointed one, would be Moses. He was the one God chose as the vessel to perform the miracles and lead the people out of Egypt, and 3. God will harden the hearts of one to control the destiny of others? As I look into my own personal life and think about Darrick, I pray that good will return to him, a heart of flesh for his heart of stone. Now, as I meditate on this scripture:

Personalize it: I realize Darrick may be where he is to effect a change in me!

Importance to my restoration/healing: Helps me to show compassion and love. Helps me to see how much I still need to grow.

Scripture I Will Own and Why: Malachi 4:6, Ezekiel 11:19; 36:26

What did you prophesy to your situation? How did you speak life?

This is how your page should look.

Allow me to explain, I put this together so I would be able to reflect. Journaling should be a road map. The journal should reflect your work in progress. It should clearly show progression. I stress that it is only effective if you are truthful about your feelings. You should be true to yourself in this journal; if you're frustrated, journal it, but include the *why*. The *why* is going to help you to find what truly upsets you. Many days, I referenced what I wrote the day before and felt I was going nowhere and then there were the days the words of a song was something I marked. One day, I

heard a song on the Kurt Franklin *Hero* CD entitled: *Afterwhile*[xii].
Here are the words to the song:

Afterwhile
(Chorus)
After a while, after a while
This too shall pass
After a while
Scars will heal, you'll love again
It won't hurt you after a while
It won't hurt after a while
(Verse 1)
Stuck between if and when
You pray and tried
But still no end
God's purpose soon you'll understand
It won't hurt you after a while
It won't hurt you after a while
(Repeat Chorus)
(Verse 2)
So when the pain has come to an end
And now your heart is whole again
Help someone who needs to know
That it won't hurt them after a while
It won't hurt them after a while
It won't hurt them after a while
(Repeat Chorus)

This song ministered to my heart. I hear it now and it reminds
me of my reconstruction and recovery.

The journal section on *point of reference* should be something you would like to reference, like what you heard or read. This could be a scripture, as in my example. It could be a passage in a book, a song, or something you heard someone say. I referenced verse 1 and 2 as it gave me strength, showing how we're able to overcome a situation. Journaling this song gave me hope. When you have a clear guide to help you journal, you're able to elaborate on what you're feeling. What I marked? Of the two passages, what did you mark or even highlight? I marked God's purpose, soon you'll understand. What it means? I journaled it and it made me sad, but it also gave me strength. Whatever the impact it had on you, write it down. Personalize it? This should be your thought, what was your initial thought when you heard or read this information, did you think of your marriage, did you have a *light bulb moment?* How did this impress you, elaborate on your thoughts? The importance to my restoration/healing? The importance to my healing, it gave me hope. I can make it if only another day.

Finally, reference a scripture you read or committed to memory. I always say the Scripture I own, because if it agrees with your Spirit, you must own it. If you own it, you will be empowered by the very mention of it. There are scriptures that I own when I am feeling low that I recite and immediately, it reminds me of the love of God. Make sure every day you journal, you "Own" your scripture. I reflect on everything, my husband, the kids, work, people that I influence, and people that I have crossed paths with. The section on the importance to my restoration, healing, or counseling: use the language you prefer. Dig a little deeper in your soul and search your deep thoughts. What impression did I leave with them? Was I loud and obnoxious, was I a reflection of God's heart, did I go the extra mile to let my family know that I love them? Did I spend my time in the presence of the Lord or was I wasteful spending time in gossip or fruitless T.V. viewing?

The journaling process is powerful, because it allows you to see how much you leaned on the Word to help you in your healing. I believe when I just simply wrote a blank page, I never had anything to fully understand and reference as I went back to read. Once I began to attack my journaling like a weapon to encourage healing, I began to see just how powerful journaling can be. I refer to my journal to see how low I was and just how God brought me out. I see how quickly God moved and how quick the devil tried to break us. I see strengths and weaknesses in my journal entries. I am able to see a pattern, which helps me to be attentive to my emotional triggers. I believe my Bible, journal, and my mouth/speech are the most powerful weapons I have. My husband is verbal, so he did not appreciate the journaling aspect, but he quickly learned how I had a point of reference with a date. He did not. I had a place to see the growth, while he did not. I had a map, a GPS if you will that he did not have and it became very apparent that he needed that reference. He began journaling and that became our *one on one* time. We shared notes; it's great to work together on your healing.

I will be honest; it was good that we didn't journal together the entire time of healing, because it would have not been notes we could share. My journals were put together almost like a book. I would joke about it being our book/our story. When friends would go through, he would say, "Honey, get "our journal". That's how this journal, our journal, became a book. Darrick began sharing my journal with neighbors and friends who thought we had the best relationship. It gave them hope. I later typed it up so we could electronically send to others. Finally, I shared with my brother and he read it for easy reading while on a flight and on his first stop, he told me, "This needs to be a book." I laughed and thought, okay. Three years later, my journal of our secret struggles became very public and the response has been amazing. I thank God because without yielding to His will, we would be amongst the divorced.

Journal Entries

Date: _____

What I Read: _____

_____

_____

What I Marked: _____

_____

_____

What it Means: _____

_____

_____

Personalize it: _____

_____

_____

Importance to My Restoration/Healing: _____

_____

_____

Scripture I Will Own and Why: _____

_____

_____

_____

What did you prophesy to your situation? How did you speak
life?_____

_____

_____

_____

Date: _____

What I Read: _____
_____
_____

What I Marked: _____
_____
_____

What it Means: _____
_____
_____

Personalize it: _____
_____
_____

Importance to My Restoration/Healing: _____
_____
_____
_____

Scripture I Will Own and Why:
_____
_____
_____
_____

What did you prophesy to your situation? How did you speak
life?_____
_____
_____
_____

Date: _____

What I Read: _____
_____
_____

What I Marked: _____
_____
_____

What it Means: _____
_____
_____

Personalize it: _____
_____
_____

Importance to My Restoration/Healing: _____
_____
_____
_____

Scripture I Will Own and Why:
_____
_____
_____
_____

What did you prophesy to your situation? How did you speak life?_____
_____
_____
_____
_____

Date: _____

What I Read: _____
_____
_____

What I Marked: _____
_____
_____

What it Means: _____
_____
_____

Personalize it: _____
_____
_____

Importance to My Restoration/Healing: _____
_____
_____
_____

Scripture I Will Own and Why:
_____
_____
_____
_____

What did you prophesy to your situation? How did you speak
life?_____
_____
_____
_____
_____

Date: _____

What I Read: _____
_____
_____

What I Marked: _____
_____
_____

What it Means: _____
_____
_____

Personalize it: _____
_____
_____

Importance to My Restoration/Healing: _____
_____
_____
_____

Scripture I Will Own and Why:
_____
_____
_____
_____

What did you prophesy to your situation? How did you speak
life?_____
_____
_____
_____
_____

Date: _____

What I Read: _____
_____
_____

What I Marked: _____
_____
_____

What it Means: _____
_____
_____

Personalize it: _____
_____
_____

Importance to My Restoration/Healing: _____
_____
_____
_____

Scripture I Will Own and Why:
_____
_____
_____
_____

What did you prophesy to your situation? How did you speak
life?_____
_____
_____
_____
_____

Date: _____

What I Read: _____
_____
_____

What I Marked: _____
_____
_____

What it Means: _____
_____
_____

Personalize it: _____
_____
_____

Importance to My Restoration/Healing: _____
_____
_____
_____

Scripture I Will Own and Why:
_____
_____
_____
_____

What did you prophesy to your situation? How did you speak
life?_____
_____
_____
_____

Date: _____

What I Read: _____
_____
_____

What I Marked: _____
_____
_____

What it Means: _____
_____
_____

Personalize it: _____
_____
_____

Importance to My Restoration/Healing: _____
_____
_____
_____

Scripture I Will Own and Why:
_____
_____
_____
_____

What did you prophesy to your situation? How did you speak life?_____
_____
_____
_____
_____

Dry Bones: God's Plan For Restoring Marriage

Date: _____

What I Read: _____
_____
_____

What I Marked: _____
_____
_____

What it Means: _____
_____
_____

Personalize it: _____
_____
_____

Importance to My Restoration/Healing: _____
_____
_____
_____

Scripture I Will Own and Why:
_____
_____
_____
_____

What did you prophesy to your situation? How did you speak
life?_____
_____
_____
_____
_____

About The Author

Nycholle Woolfolk-Gater has spent her life walking the path that the Lord has set before her, touching the hearts of many, and helping a few find their own. Now, as a resource specialist, she supports veterans by uncovering benefits and programs that they are in need of and provides caregiver coaching to their spouses and family members.

Nycholle is married to Darrick E. Gater and they share six children together: Brittany, Amber, Colby, Devin, Eugene, and Ben, and their grandchildren Kingston and Tristan.

Bibliography

[i] *The Bible's Teaching on Marriage and the Family* by Andreas Kostenberger. Retrieved on http://www.frc.org/brochure/the-bibles-teaching-on-marriage-and-family.

[ii] Omartian, Stormie. *The Power of a Praying Wife.* (Harvest House Publishers, Eugene, OR). Published 2000.

[iii] Yandian, Bob. *One Flesh: God's Gift of Passion-Love, Sex & Romance in Marriage.* (Creation House, Lake Mary, FL). Published 1996.

[iv] Chapman, Gary. *The Five Love Languages.* (Lifeway Press, Nashville, TN). Published 2007.

[v] *Business News Daily polled 15 Great Entrepreneurs* by Tom Kennedy. https://www.businessnewsdaily.com/3269-how-to-be-a-leader.html.

[vi] Duke, Bill. "(Producer)". (2009) *Not Easily Broken.* Based upon the book *Not Easily Broken* by Jakes, T.D. (FaithWords, A Division of Hatchette Book Group, Nashville, TN). Published 2007.

[vii] Fulghum, Robert. *All I Really Need to Know I Learned in Kindergarten: Uncommon Thoughts on Uncommon Things.* (Ballentine Books, New York City, NY). Published 2004.

[viii] Nolte, Dorothy Law. *Children Learn What They Live* (Poem). (Published 1954)

[ix] Estimated at 7.13 billion people as of 2013.
http://www.worldometers.info/world-population/.

[x] Bible *Woman Thou Art Loosed Edition*. Editor T.D. Jakes.
(Thomas Nelson Publishers, Nashville, TN). Published 2003.

[xi] Arterburn, Stephen and Merrill, Dean. *Every Man's Bible, A Bible for Every Battle Every Man Faces*. (Tyndale House Publishers, Carol Stream, IL). Published 2014.

[xii] Franklin, Kirk. "Afterwhile." 2005. *Hero*. By Writer Kirk Franklin. Perf. Kirk Franklin and Yolanda Adams. *Sony Legacy*. Rec. October 4, 2005. Producer Kirk Franklin and J Moss, 2005. CD.

www.ingramcontent.com/pod-product-compliance
Lightning Source LLC
LaVergne TN
LVHW051409080426
835508LV00022B/3006